# BOLD AND BROKEN

# DAVID AND JASON BENHAM

# BOLD AND BROKEN

## BECOMING THE BRIDGE BETWEEN HEAVEN AND EARTH

SALEMBOOKS
an imprint of Regnery Publishing

Regnery® is a registered trademark of Salem Communications Holding Corporation

Salem Books™ is a trademark of Salem Communications Holding Corporation

Cataloging-in-Publication data on file with the Library of Congress

ISBN: 978-1-62157-916-8
Ebook ISBN: 978-1-62157-917-5

Library of Congress Cataloging-in-Publication Data

Published in the United States by
Salem Books, an imprint of
Regnery Publishing
A Division of Salem Media Group
300 New Jersey Ave NW
Washington, DC 20001
www.Regnery.com

Manufactured in the United States of America

10 9 8 7 6 5 4 3 2 1

Published in association with the literary agency of WTA Services LLC, Franklin, TN.

Books are available in quantity for promotional or premium use. For information on discounts and terms, please visit our website: www.Regnery.com

# TABLE OF CONTENTS

# INTRODUCTION

**D**o you ever have conversations with God? Like, real conversations where you ask Him questions and wait for a response? I (Jason) had one I'll never forget.

I was outside praying early one morning. The sun had not yet risen. Even the birds were still asleep. As I paced back and forth in the cool morning breeze, looking up at the stars every so often, I asked the Holy Spirit to speak to me.

On this particular morning, I was thinking and praying about this book you hold in your hands. "What do you want us to say?" I asked the Spirit, fully expecting Him to roll back the black sky like a scroll and download the entire manuscript right then and there.

*Crickets.*

That's all I heard at that moment. The gentle, constant hum of crickets.

But I didn't want to hear crickets—I wanted to hear the voice of God! I wanted Him to give me the cosmic download with every word for every chapter unfolded before my watching eye. But that's not what happened.

My spirit began to grow anxious, as I heard nothing for what seemed like hours. It was more like minutes, really.

As is my typical routine, I laid on my back in the driveway, facing the stars. Thoughts about how Jesus prayed under this same sky and saw many of those same stars flooded my mind. It gave me a sense of connection to Him. It felt good, like a warm blanket on a cold day. Even better, a hot cup of tea in the dead of winter. It was warmth from the inside-out.

Every now and then I had to fight off the wandering thought, "I bet David is drooling on his pillow right now." I later discovered, he was up too, praying about the exact same thing.

Then it happened. I heard the Lord speak to me, "*Stand—In—The—Gap.*" It wasn't an audible voice like you and me talking with each other, but a faint whisper in my spirit, guiding me, saying, "This is the way."

At first, I thought it was just the memory of the voices from friends who told us we needed to write a book on the topic. Neither one of us felt compelled to do that. But as it persisted, I knew it was the Holy Spirit prompting me to think more deeply.

*Okay*, I thought, remembering back to a verse I read where God told Ezekiel He was looking for someone who would stand in the gap for Him on behalf of the land. *I get that.* God is looking for people who will stand strong for Him (Ezekiel 22:30).

I understand we live in a time when the fundamental truths under-girding civil society are being redefined at breakneck speed. Many people are doing what is right in their own eyes. And the result is not the freedom and connection people long for but frustration and disconnection that leaves them feeling empty. Chaos fills that gap. And the longer the gap remains, the more hurting people will remain in their pain.

If there were ever a time for Christians to step up and stand in the gap, bringing hope to the hopeless, now is that time.

But because we were fired by HGTV in 2014 for our Biblical values, we've been traveling the country encouraging Christians to stand in this gap—to be courageous in a compromised culture. And we've written books before that shared our views. "Why would we need to write another one?" I asked.

As I lay there talking with God I felt like He wanted to say more.

So, I waited. And waited. And waited.

Then a thought popped into my head to pray the Lord's Prayer. Was this my thought or was it God? I had no clue at the time. It felt like it was mine, but because Jesus told His disciples to pray that way, I knew better than to question the impulse.

I simply moved in that direction. "Our Father," I prayed slowly, thinking deeply so it didn't become a simple religious routine. "Who art in Heaven, hallowed be your name. Your kingdom come, Your will be done, on earth as it is in heaven."

"Stop!" I heard the Holy Spirit say. "This phrase—'*on earth as it is in heaven*'—meditate on it."

*But how does this have anything to do with standing in the gap*, I wondered.

Fighting off the thought, *can you please give me more than that*, I stood to my feet and started pacing, reciting this phrase over and over and over.

The more I repeated it, the more I began to see there is a divine disconnect between heaven and earth—a spiritual gap between God and man. And He taught us to pray that it be reconnected.

The more I considered, this the more I realized this isn't just about prayer—it's about participation. God wants us to participate in His reconnection process between heaven and earth, between Him and the people He's created. We do this by standing in the gap between the two.

I think by this time I went from slowly pacing to Olympic speed walking. I felt energized by what God was showing me in this divine moment where every ounce of confusion was met with amazing clarity. This book was not only to simply encourage believers to stand in the gap but also to show what we *become* when we do—a vital connection between God and people.

We—the people God created in His image and made whole through Christ—are part of His sovereign plan to make this connection, to fill the spiritual gap that exists because of sin. Of course, Jesus was the ultimate connection through His death on the cross—but now He uses *us* to continue the connection. He works *through* us to do His work. As Hudson Taylor, the famous Chinese missionary, said, "God's work is not man working for God; it is God's own work, though often wrought through man's hands." This is why Jesus taught us to pray as He did.

When we stand in the gap for others, we connect them to God—*on earth as it is in heaven*. But this isn't for the faint of heart. There's a very real enemy who wants nothing more than to leave that gaping hole just like it is, and he knows exactly how to target us to keep us out of it.

It takes boldness to connect others to God. But boldness alone won't get the job done. Boldness apart from brokenness makes a bully. You can stand with courage, but without compassion, you'll only widen the gap.

At the same time, brokenness apart from boldness makes a bystander. You can be the most compassionate person on the planet, but without courage, the result is the same widening gap.

When you're bold *and* broken you become a bridge—one connecting heaven to earth in supernatural ways. When you stand in the gap courageously for God with a heart of compassion for others, you become the answer to Christ's prayer—*on earth as it is in heaven*.

Within these pages, we're going to show you what it looks like to stand in the gap and become that bridge in real, practical ways. We'll dive into the characteristics that illustrate that sacred and joy-filled calling of manifesting God's will on earth. We'll share our stories as well as those of ordinary men and women who had moments when they became an indispensable connection between God and people.

From mothers praying at the grocery store and high schoolers preaching in the lunchroom to teachers sharing in the classroom and businessmen witnessing on airplanes, the stories in this book will show how seemingly small and insignificant people became strong and indispensable connections God used to draw people back to Himself.

You will probably find yourself in many of these stories because they might be just like yours— moments when divine connection happened and moments when, well, maybe not so much. You may be surprised by what you hear. By reading these stories, it will help you shape your story as it fits into *His*tory.

As you read, you'll be encouraged and equipped to stand in the gap, too. And when you do, you'll experience the joy from knowing with certainty you're right where God wants you to be—a bridge connecting heaven to earth.

The time to stand in the gap is NOW! People are suffering. Cultures are caving. The gap is wider than ever. And God is calling YOU. Will you stand? Will you be that bridge between heaven and earth?

We think you will. It's not going to be easy. But it will certainly be worth it.

Let's get started. Go grab a cup of coffee (or protein shake) and let us take you back to a time when standing in the gap looked a lot like front-row tickets to a Chicago Cubs baseball game.

# CHAPTER 1

# CHICAGO

A few days after we lost our reality show and our faces were plastered all over social media, we received a private message on Facebook from a man in Chicago. At this point, we had been called pretty much every name in the book, most of which can't be mentioned in this one. The clash between our voice for Biblical values and the culture's vitriol against them was brutal. It certainly didn't bring out the best in some people, especially our newfound Chicago friend. He was extremely mad at us. Come to think of it, mad is an understatement. He was furious.

The venom this man was spewing as he ripped into us turned our stomachs upside down. Initially, we both felt the knee-jerk reaction to boldly defend and debate. We grew up fighters, so we have no problem locking horns. And as twins, fighting is in our DNA—though we mostly fight with each other.

## YEAH, WE FIGHT A LITTLE

If you've ever heard us speak, you've most likely seen this in action. We have no issue sparring verbally right there on stage in front of everyone. Once, we were in Connecticut speaking at a men's conference, and this nice, older gentleman came up to me (Jason) and said, "I was just thinking about the way you guys jab at each other. Maybe you should try a different approach."

Intrigued by his idea of a better approach I asked him to tell me what I should say. "Here's what I would do," he said, "I'd put my arm around him and tell the crowd, 'This is my brother, and I want you all to know what a gift of God he is.'"

Uh—I just need to say right now—there's not a chance in the WORLD that's going to happen—ever! After I fought back the nausea that idea provoked, I jokingly said, "Maybe I'll try that sometime."

When I told David later, he erupted in laughter. Because he knows I'm a bit of a prankster, he got serious for a minute and said, "If you ever do that to me I'll drop you in front of everyone." That would be a speaking engagement nobody would ever forget.

Dad raised us to be fighters, in every sense of the term. When we were kids, he loved to watch us box. For Christmas each year, we'd buy each other Sugar Ray Leonard boxing gloves. We'd pull them from under the tree and, like clockwork, we'd start wailing on each other while Dad shadow-boxed the air as he watched us.

We'd hear mom in the background, "Flip, stop them! They're being too rough."

"Nah, this is good for them," he'd tell her as he threw a phantom left jab while holding his right hand by his face. "They need to learn how to defend themselves."

I guess now would be a good time to tell you David's defense was never as good as mine. When we were fourteen years old, I dropped him in a backyard boxing match with a lightning-fast jab to the chin. What an incredible feeling that was. He lost control of his temper and wound up to hit me, but when he did he left himself wide open for a knockout blow. I caught his chin and dropped him like a bag of bricks. When he regained consciousness, he started screaming, "All I see is green!" It was the most amazing feeling a boy could ever have. My eyes still well up with tears of joy thinking about that moment.

It was this desire to fight we felt when we got that message from the man in Chicago. *We've got to defend ourselves,* we thought as we poised to correct the false perception this guy had about us. By this time our reputations were smeared in the mud of recriminations, so our gut response was to go back to those backyard bouts and take care of business—verbally.

Of course, at that moment we weren't thinking of Christ's words when He said we're blessed when people falsely accuse us (Matthew 5:11).

Within seconds, the Holy Spirit checked our boldness and reminded us of brokenness, bringing that beautiful balance only the Spirit can bring. Our hearts broke for this man because we were reminded of our own past sin issues and how merciful God was with us.

At that moment we didn't need to win our point, we needed to win a person. This man's argument against us did not represent a fight to win but a person to love. And we couldn't do this without first walking in brokenness.

So, we responded, "We see you're upset at us, but what we know is that you're simply speaking through your pain."

He must have been on Facebook at the same time because within minutes he shot back what seemed like the longest response in Facebook Messenger history. He basically dumped his life story on us, and with every word we read, our hearts grieved even more for him.

This was a man who was disconnected from the God who created him, loved him, and had a wonderful plan for him. He had a daddy-gap that could be filled only by his Heavenly Father. God crossed our paths so we could be a part of standing in that gap.

With hearts full of compassion for this man, we engaged in conversation, telling him how God radically transformed our own lives because He loves us and wants what's best for us, and He could do the same for him. We then explained how God loves him just like he is but refuses to leave him that way—because He's too good a God to leave us like we are, captured by our sin.

We've got to be honest here. Telling him that last part—God had something better for him than his current lifestyle—was not easy. When our hearts broke for him, we didn't want to hurt his feelings in any way or turn him off. But, we knew God had the answer to his current situation, and he needed to hear it. We were already convicted of being bold bullies, but now we were tempted to be broken bystanders. Fortunately, the Holy Spirit working in us was able to bring the balance.

Interestingly, in the course of the conversation, we discovered this guy was an avid Chicago Cubs fan. Prompted by the Lord, we told him we wanted to get two front row tickets for him and a friend to a Cubs game at Wrigley Field.

There's simply nothing like smashing a ballpark dog on game day at Wrigley when the Cardinals are in town. Seriously, if you haven't done it, put that on your bucket list.

The man was gracious in his response, thanking us for being willing to buy him tickets, but he refused. We pressed, "Come on man—let us send you and friend to the game. You'll love it!"

What he said next ripped our hearts out. "I don't have any friends."

Can you imagine how difficult it was for him to write those five words? It's even hard to write this now without feeling deep emotion for him. Here's a man who was once a boy with a mom who loved him, friends who liked him, and hopes and dreams of what he wanted to be one day. Now, he was just a broken man void of hope and the deep relationships none of us can survive without.

We pressed in a bit more, and he finally agreed to go to the game, alone.

A few days later, he sent us a message with these words, "Thank you so much for what you did. I've been listening to this song [he sent a link to Mercy Me's song, "I Can Only Imagine"], and I've decided to leave my lifestyle and turn back to God."

What?! It's never that simple—but God had been working on this guy's heart all along, narrowing the gap between heaven and earth in his heart. All he needed was a little more love, and God used Cubs tickets and a Mercy Me song to seal the deal! It was amazing to be a part of God's work in this man's life.

This guy's story is just one small example of the gaps in our culture—gaping holes created by the demonic forces of this world that seek to maintain control over the people God created in His image. You probably know of a few of them right now who, like him, need a bridge back to their Creator to experience the abundant life only He can give. The question is: Will we be that bridge for the guy in Chicago, for those around us, for a nation in desperate need?

It was our assignment that day with our Chicago friend. And it's our assignment every day as God opens doors for us to connect His will to man's ways, on earth as it is in heaven. The more deliberately we look for those assignments, the more we will see how others have been carrying them out for years, and with some startling results. Take, for instance, a man named after a hot dog.

CHAPTER 2

# FERT

He looked like the leader of a biker gang, only without the leather jacket. As he walked toward us, we noticed his long brown hair was pulled back in a ponytail. The closer he got, the more visible the raunchy tattoos were on his arm—the kind our mom would have covered our eyes from when we were boys. He had a fierce look about him that said, "Cross me, I will bury you alive and still sleep like a baby."

Okay, so being buried alive has always been one of our weird phobias. It probably has something to do with a movie we saw when we were kids: A guy was put in a wooden box and dropped in a hole while another covered it with dirt. Maybe.

Seeing a guy like this at a church picnic caught us a little off guard. But, by the time he was a few feet away, his hardened-criminal appearance wasn't quite so intimidating. His smile was so big you'd think somebody poked his ticklish spot. His eyes held a joy that made you think, "What have you seen and can you take me there?"

As he extended his hand of greeting, he bellowed in a gruff northeastern accent, "Hey, you guys know Pastor Frank?"

Frank was the chaplain of our summer baseball team in Torrington, Connecticut, that year. We finished our junior year at Liberty and were invited to play in a college wooden-bat league in New England. I (Jason) later fell in love with his daughter, and now he's my father-in-law. Lucky guy.

Frank invited us to the picnic during that summer season.

7

"You mean Fert? Sure!" we responded. (We nicknamed Frank "Fert," as in the hot dog *frankfurter*—only spelled with an "e"). "How do you know him?"

"Awww, Frank? Everyone knows Frank," he said, grabbing us both by our arms and grinning. "He changed my life, that guy."

Just as our heads were starting to clear from shock, another dude walked up. He had his hair back in a ponytail too and was wearing a tight t-shirt displaying the results of his talent for picking up heavy things and putting them down. The two men looked like twins—not because of their physical appearance but because they both had massive smiles and bright, joy-filled eyes.

"I'm Jeff," he said shaking our hands. "How do you know my brother, Phil?"

"Didn't even know his name was Phil," we said. "We just met him."

"These are Frank's buddies," Phil said.

"Awww, Frank!" Jeff replied in the same deep northeastern accent as his brother. "He changed my life, that guy."

We were going to ask how Frank changed their lives, but then a modern-day Goliath walked up and arrested our attention.

"This is Big Ed," Jeff said heartily. We waited for him to finish with, *and he'll be burying you both alive in a box after the picnic!*

Big Ed was a giant lumberjack of a man. He had red hair and hands the size of toaster ovens. We felt like little Marty McFly in the movie *Back to the Future* when big-boy Biff pushed him up against the car, only this guy had the same smile and brightness in his eyes as Jeff and Phil.

"Frank knows these guys, Big Ed," Phil said.

"Awww, Frank!" Big Ed replied, nodding.

We had a feeling what was coming next. Sure enough, the next line out of his mouth was, "He changed my life, that guy."

And for the next thirty minutes, these three former hooligans told us how Frank changed the trajectory of their lives forever. Every one of them served time in jail and was headed in the wrong direction, but because of the faithful witness of one man, everything changed.

## FRANK'S POSSE

Phil, Jeff, and Big Ed told us about the weekly men's meeting Frank led at church for a bunch of ex-ruffians who came from backgrounds of illegal drugs, alcohol, sex, and crime. They had the scars to prove it. We got to meet a lot of those guys that summer. You could tell by how they looked, these guys once led rough lives, but every one of them beamed from the inside. They were so filled with joy and love, it emanated from them.

For these guys, Frank was a friend, mentor, life coach, pastor, marriage counselor, and whatever else they needed him to be. He filled a gap in their lives and brought a divine connection that made him a powerful link between them and God.

These guys loved Frank. It's good having friends like him in your corner. Frank told us later about a time when he took them all to a conference where a charismatic pastor was praying for people down front. One by one the people at the altar fell over when the pastor touched them. As the pastor made his way down the line toward Frank, Phil and the guys stepped in front of him and made a wall so the pastor couldn't touch him. They weren't about to let their spiritual dad hit the deck. They stood there in a "not on our watch" position until the pastor passed over them and continued down the line.

Frank missed the anointing that could've been his that night, but he received another kind of blessing altogether. He was a bridge to God for this group of men. Even though he was the same age as many of them, he became their spiritual father, pouring into their lives as God poured into his.

## GET IN THE GAME

Frank became the same for several of us players that summer as the chaplain for our baseball team. When we played professional baseball, it was tough getting guys to come to chapel but not when we were in Torrington with Frank as the leader. All the guys loved him.

One teammate, in particular, was a big fan of Frank's. Ryan was a pitcher from Massachusetts with a thick "Bawston" accent. But most of the time, the accent was drowned out by his frequent profanity. He had more stuff flying out of him than we ever heard from any teammate—ever.

Ryan eventually started coming to chapel with us, and Frank took a special interest in helping him. Looking back, we think Frank saw himself in Ryan. He poured himself into Ryan that summer, and slowly but surely, all of us could see a visible change in this once-hardened ball player. He actually smiled a lot, and he'd go an entire inning, or maybe even two, without dropping any bombs (that's lingo for using profanity).

His mouth cleaned up really well, that is, until the last game of the season when we got into a bench-clearing brawl with the other team. It's a long story, so we won't go into the details, but suffice it to say one of their players ran over our catcher and put him in the hospital, so the handshake at the end of the game didn't end well.

We were with Frank down on the field trying to stop the fight. We saw Ryan wailing on a guy as expletives flew out of his mouth like bats flying out of a cave. Frank ran over and grabbed the back of his shirt and pulled him off the dude. Ryan looked back, "Oh, hey Pastor Frank," he said, startled. "You didn't hear what I just said, did you?"

You know you're a person of influence when others feel a weight of conviction simply by your presence. Frank was God's representative to Ryan and the rest of the team better than any chaplain we ever had.

Frank had some of the best quotes too. He used to say, "Boys, God wants to use the uniqueness of you to present the uniqueness of Him." We didn't realize how powerful a thought that was until later in life. But it's true—God doesn't want you to become anyone else. He wants you to be *you*, and He will use you as He sees fit. You just need to be available, like Fert.

He was a spiritual father to many. He was also the unelected mayor of Torrington and the unappointed pastor of the city. Everybody knew him, loved him, and respected him.

## FATHERS

Fert's life reminds us of what Paul spoke about in his letter to the church at Corinth, a city in desperate need of *spiritual fathers* who were willing to stand in the gap. "You have many teachers," Paul said, "but few fathers" (1 Corinthians 4:15).

Frank's earthly father was a quintessential Italian whose parents came off the boat in New York City harbor from Italy. Jake was his name. My (Jason's) second son is named after him.

Now, when we say Italian, we mean *Italian,* like a person you'd see in the movie *Godfather.* Jake (or *Poppie* as his grandkids called him) didn't take anything from anyone. He could out-argue anyone at any time, too, and in typical Italian fashion, he was always open for the challenge.

He was a hard-working man who worked his fingers to the bone to provide a good life for his family, and he expected Frank to do the same.

When Frank was in high school, he was in the hospital recovering from knee surgery when he called his mom to see if she could bring him an Italian grinder (that's an Italian version of a sub sandwich).

Oh no, we shouldn't have mentioned grinders. Our mouths are starting to water. Connecticut has some of the absolute best hole-in-the-wall Italian delis around. They put more meat on their sandwiches than you could possibly stuff into your mouth. All the good meat too, not that fake stuff you get at the grocery store. They've got that small-town feel when you walk in and hear the little bell on the door as you're greeted by the smell of fresh-baked bread and a host of "Howya doins?" from the back. Gotta love it.

Grinders were Frank's favorite, so he asked his mom to get him one. But he jokingly said if she didn't get him one, he'd jump out the window.

When she told his dad, he responded, "Let him jump. He's on the first floor."

To give you a little glimpse of Frank's family life growing up, think of the movie "My Big Fat Greek Wedding." With an Italian dad, a Polish mom, and a son who knew how to push all their buttons, they had some of the most epic battles you could imagine. We still roar in laughter at the stories.

## MAN ON A MISSION

Poppie was a hardcore Italian and raised Frank in the Catholic church. So, when Frank became a Christian at twenty years old and started going to an evangelical church, it didn't sit too well with his dad. Poppie made Frank feel he as though he chose a relationship with Jesus over a relationship with the family. For years Frank tried to bridge that gap. They had an amazing relationship as father and son, but he wanted desperately to lead his dad to salvation in Jesus. Poppie, on the other hand, felt like Frank was pulled away from his family to join another. Although Poppie would never admit it, he was hurt deep inside.

We remember Frank telling us the one thing he wanted more than anything was for his entire family to meet Jesus, especially his dad. His mission in life revolved around this single goal. And for twenty-six years, he tried and prayed.

Then one day he got a phone call—his dad had terminal lung cancer.

By that time, Frank's daughter Tori and I (Jason) were married. I remember walking through this with their family. It was hard to watch Poppie walk around with an oxygen tank connected to a tube in his nose. He wasn't the man I remembered the few summers before—a man who never let me forget about a special pair of pliers in his garage he saved just for me in case I ever hurt his granddaughter.

He never lost his quick wit. On one of his doctor's visits, a nurse was filling out his paperwork and asked him if he wanted to be an organ donor. Without hesitation, he said, "Yea, my lungs to Osama Bin Laden."

The news of Poppie's sickness hit Frank especially hard. He didn't want to lose his dad. More importantly, he wanted to make sure he would be in Heaven when he died.

For the next nine months, all of us watched the most amazing display of what a man on a mission looks like. Frank hardly left his dad's side, picking him up for appointments, taking him to the store, sitting with him at the diner so he could enjoy coffee with his buddies—whatever it was, Frank was there to help his dad. And all along the way, he had one central goal—to love his dad to Jesus.

The cancer moved fast. Faster than we all thought it would. Frank flew in to see Tori and me in Charlotte, North Carolina, for a few days when he got a call. I'll never forget the call because Frank and I took a helicopter trip with a buddy of ours. Before we took off, he slipped me three Dramamine but didn't tell me what they were. "Here, these will help you not get sick," he told me.

Thirty minutes later in the helicopter, I was a drooling mess in a near-comatose state. When the ride was over, he had to carry me back to our apartment where I laid on the couch. I could hear him laughing hysterically at me, but I was too tired to do anything about it.

But the laughs ended abruptly when Tori told him to call her mom. She informed him Poppie took a turn for the worse, was in the hospital, and might not make it through the night.

Frank quickly gathered his stuff and took off to the airport, hoping and praying he'd get there before his dad passed away. When he got to the hospital, the nurse asked him if he was Frankie. She said his dad kept asking for him and said, "I need to see Frankie."

When Frank walked into his dad's room, he saw Poppie there, barely hanging on to life. "I'm all done, kid," his dad said. With a grey haze in his eyes, he looked at Frank and asked, "Did you know it was this bad?"

"No, dad," Frank responded. "I didn't know it would happen this quickly."

"So tell me what I gotta do," Poppie said.

Sensing the urgency of the moment, Frank advised, "You gotta talk to Ma—tell her everything you want to say. Then talk to Dootie." Dootie was Frank's sister.

One at a time, Frank's mom and sister went into the room and said their tearful goodbyes.

Finally, it was Frank's turn. Knowing this would most likely be the last time he'd get to talk to his dad, and with tears streaming down his cheeks, Frank said, "Dad, can I pray with you?"

"Not this time," Poppie said as he slowly took his oxygen mask off. "I've got this one, kid."

"Jesus, forgive me of my sins," he said in a faint voice. "And let Frankie know that my heart is not hollow or empty but filled with Jesus. And help him be the man he needs to be for the family."

Four hours later, Jake Cantadore entered the gates of Heaven.

## BE THE BRIDGE

Do you want to know what being a bridge looks like? It looks like a man who not only rose to being a father in his church and city but one who also became a spiritual father to his earthly father. It looks like a man willing to pursue the heart of his dad right up to his dying day in efforts to see his soul saved—a man who prayed and prayed and prayed until God answered that prayer just in the nick of time.

Maybe you have loved ones who don't know Jesus. Quite possibly you've been praying and pursuing them like Frank did his dad, but nothing has happened. Don't give up! You keep standing in that gap. You never know, maybe on their dying day they'll whisper, "My heart is not hollow or empty; it's filled with Jesus."

CHAPTER 3

# MEET ME ON A JET PLANE

**W**ould you think differently of us if we told you when we get on a plane together we hope nobody sits between us? Even though planes rides can lead to the most rewarding spiritual conversations, it's a consistent battle for us to actually *want* to do it. Plane time is snooze time, right? Our hearts might want to create that heaven/earth connection, but sometimes our bodies just want that snooze.

There's nothing like the feeling of utter exhaustion when you grab your window seat in row eight and in plops a chatter-box who hasn't gotten his (or her) 20,000 words in yet. Not to mention he's at 12,000 and counting but failed to do anything about the stale breath that just screams, "I hate gum."

In those moments, the temptation is to pray, "Lord, you once put a spirit of deep sleep on Saul in the Old Testament—you can do it again. Would you mind helping out our friend in the middle seat?"

But we know whoever sits in the seat between us was put there by God, and it's our assignment to talk to him as the Lord leads. Because we're twins we take turns. Typically, just before we walk onto the plane, one of us will lean over to the other and say, "You've got it this time." This is code for "It's your responsibility to talk to the person in the middle seat."

God has shown us that if you wait to minister to someone until you have a desire to do it, you probably won't. You must simply go for it and the desire will come on the other end. Action precedes motivation. If you wait until you *feel* like doing something, you might never do it.

We can take it to the bank that if we feel exhausted before a flight but still choose to engage someone during the flight, we always feel energized after the flight. Only the Holy Spirit can do something that amazing.

And God has a sense of humor. He knows just how to test our limits.

## SNOOZE AND LOSE

A few years ago, we boarded a plane in Dallas, Texas, headed back home to Charlotte. As usual, we were exhausted. The plane was only half full, so there were plenty of open seats (nobody in the middle!). David and I each had aisle seats with an entire row to ourselves. We could hear the angels singing.

But, as the last passengers boarded the plane a young, college-aged girl came and took the window seat on my (Jason's) row. Let me just tell ya—she was a talker! During the chatter, I felt that familiar battle inside my heart. Part of me cried, "Why couldn't her seat have been next to my idiot brother?!" But the Holy Spirit whispered, "Talk to her—I have a message for her, and I want to give it through you."

I knew what the Holy Spirit wanted me to do. I was just so tired. During my internal battle just before takeoff, the flight attendant came up to me and said, "There's an exit row a few rows up that's vacant. Would you like to take it?"

Uh, do bears poop in the woods? "Of course I'll take it," I said with a smile.

Without a second thought, I got up and settled into my new row all by myself. Just before I dozed off I felt that little nudge from the Spirit again. I knew God wanted me to talk with her and bring the spiritual connection she might have needed, but my head was hurting and my eyes were heavy. I needed sleep, you know—I wanted to be refreshed for the kids when I got home—don't judge me! The excuses were endless.

I slept the entire flight home.

As I got off the plane in Charlotte and walked up the jet bridge, I saw the girl in the distance, waiting by the gate agent desk. I have no clue how she got ahead of me. All I know is she looked like she wanted to say something to me.

By the time I got where she was, she looked me right in the eye and said, "Hey, why did you take off like that? I had a lot to talk about." Then she turned around with a smile and walked away.

I'm not sure if she was joking or serious, but I've never seen her since to find out.

The minute she said that, I felt an instant prick in my heart. I was given an assignment, and I 100% refused to do it.

The Lord used her words to rebuke me. I mean, how many young girls say something like that to a forty-plus-year-old man? God got my attention. "The Lord disciplines the one he loves, and he chastens everyone He accepts as his son" (Hebrews 12:6).

The entire ride home I felt guilty. But repentance changes everything. I asked God to forgive me and bring someone else into her life who would listen to what she had to say. I also asked Him to give me another chance, and a few months later He did.

## FIGHT IN FLIGHT

Before Jason got a chance to redeem himself from his epic fail, he and I flew to St. Louis, Missouri, to speak at a pro-life event. I (David) was on the aisle, and Jason got the window. That left the middle seat open for one lucky (or unlucky) person.

I settled into my seat and opened my Bible to study a bit before take-off. Then an older woman came up said she had the seat between us. I noticed she was holding a book with a picture of Donald Trump and a bunch of red letters scribbled all over the cover. I couldn't read what was written, but it didn't look favorable toward him. It was obvious her preferred reading for that flight was quite different from mine.

I stood up and helped her to her seat, and after a little small talk, she looked at me and said, "I just want you to know I'm a flaming liberal feminist who probably thinks nothing like you."

Wow!—now *that's* a great way to engage a conversation. It felt like she smacked me in the teeth without even getting my name. And she looked back and forth at Jason and me while she said it as if to declare, "I'm going to take you *both* down!"

I'm pretty sure it was my Bible that sparked a rise in her, as it has a few times before on other flights.

I'm sure Jason would have been intimidated by what she said if he wasn't already ugly-face snoozing on the window. But I was locked in and ready to engage. In my mind, I was going to dismantle her worldview piece by piece, proving how a Biblical value system was better than a secular one. But I couldn't stop thinking about how abrupt she was and what in her life would've caused her to be so confrontational. My head was ready for conflict, but my heart was pricked with compassion.

I paused a second and whispered a quick prayer for wisdom. I felt the Holy Spirit compel me to ask her questions about her life and family rather than engage in a debate over our different views.

"So, tell me about yourself," I said.

She was clearly caught off guard. I think she had put on her fight face and was ready to duke it out.

"Oh," she said as her fists slowly went down. "I'm married with two kids and am flying home to be with them."

She then carried on for twenty straight minutes about her family—what they liked to do for fun, how she and her daughter are just like each other, the time her husband caught a big fish on vacation. I didn't even have to ask more questions. She continued talking and then shifted from telling less about the fun things they've done to more about their struggles.

I just sat there and listened. The more I listened, the more I realized there was a gap in her life that needed to be filled so she could connect with God. At that moment, she didn't need me to change her mind—she needed me to hear her heart. The Lord was about to have an encounter with her.

She eventually told me her son was struggling with depression and anxiety and how it weighed heavy on her. She was also transitioning into a new season in her life, which brought some anxiety for her as well.

I felt a nudge in my spirit say, "Read Psalm 139."

I asked, "Do you mind if I share a verse with you?"

"Sure," she responded. It's funny how quick and emphatic her response was. Twenty minutes earlier, I'm fairly certain she would've laughed in my face had I asked to read a Bible verse to her.

I opened to Psalm 139 and began reading.

> For You formed my inward parts;
> You wove me in my mother's womb.
> I will give thanks to You, for I am fearfully and wonder-
> fully made;
> Wonderful are Your works,
> And my soul knows it very well.
> My frame was not hidden from You,
> When I was made in secret,
> And skillfully wrought in the depths of the earth;
> Your eyes have seen my unformed substance;
> And in Your book were all written
> The days that were ordained for me,
> When as yet there was not one of them.
> How precious also are Your thoughts to me, O God!
> How vast is the sum of them! (Psalms 139:13–7)

In the middle of my reading, her chin began to quiver, and soon tears were flowing down her cheeks. I watched her wipe them away while I read. God was speaking directly to her—more than any words I could have formed on my own. At that moment, heaven was invading earth—God was connecting with her in a very real way. It was surreal to watch the Lord move so profoundly. I felt honored to be part of the moment.

I figured I'd better keep reading the rest of the chapter—I didn't really know what else to do—but she stopped me after verse seventeen. "It's weird I'm telling you this," she said as she took out a tissue. "But I was adopted as a newborn and have always felt abandoned by my birth mom. I still have recurring dreams of me at the hospital as a baby, lying in a crib and saying to myself (like an adult would speak), 'Nobody needs to feel sorry for me—I'll take care of myself!'"

It was amazing. She got right to the root of her feminism without me saying a single word about it.

With tears still streaming down her face, she released all that had been pent up in her for years. God's word softened her as she began to see how much He cared for her, thought about her, and was with her the whole time she felt so alone. His truth warmed her heart and began melting away the icy coldness built up over the years.

I even started to cry, which is odd for me, as I told her how Jesus had the power to break the chains of abandonment, fear, and anxiety. I shared other Scriptures with her as well and encouraged her to place her trust in God as her Father. She was so touched by the verses, she even pulled out her phone and began making notes about them.

Just before the plane landed, Jason finally woke up from his open-mouthed sleep and joined the conversation. It was nice of him to at least help a little. By the time we pulled up to the gate, she was a completely different woman. The angry, independent, fighter front turned into a loving, caring, nurturer. She became so motherly as she asked us about our kids and took a real interest in our families.

The presence of God visited us on the plane that day, and it marked us all. Heaven touched earth. A connection between God and one of His kids took place. This woman who was *bamwiched* between us (that's a "Benham sandwich," in case you didn't know) left transformed with healing in her heart and a new song in her mouth.

If it were up to me that day, I would have missed this golden opportunity to be a bridge for her to God. I was ready to fight and win. But in so doing, I might have proved a point, but I would have lost a person. Thank God the Holy Spirit stopped me in my tracks and shifted my focus.

## DOG DAY

On the flight home from that amazing St. Louis flight and still feeling the sting of that missed opportunity from the Dallas flight, I (Jason) got another opportunity. This time, it involved a woman in the middle seat who had a dog the size of two laptops. This little guy was brown and short, like a weenie dog. I think they call them Dachshunds.

When she sat between David and me, I instantly had two emotions. The first was a flashback to growing up next to our neighbor who had two of these dogs. Useless animals, I thought as a kid—what could they really accomplish, other than annoying neighbors with constant yelping?

These kinds of dogs run like my 90-year-old grandmother (who's actually not too shabby on the treadmill now that she's got two new knees). They have zero ability to protect. And they shed, which makes them off limits for anyone with the last name Benham. I was pretty bitter about the dog, but I guess they do keep people company, which is a good thing, no doubt.

I wasn't sure if I should be thankful for the fact the butt-end of the dog was facing my direction while his tail consistently thumped down on my leg every fifteen seconds, or if I would prefer the front-end where he licked David's hand every sixty seconds. Either way, both of us had ninety minutes with this thing—and there was no way out.

"I've got to power through it," I thought, wiping away the tiny hairs falling on my pants. It seemed like every time I brushed them away more would appear. At some point, I just stopped wiping. By the time the flight was over, I was covered with dog hair. Nice. There was so much hair on me I'm surprised he had any left.

I knew it was my turn to strike up a conversation, though, because this was the return leg of the trip where David had that amazing encounter with the "flaming, liberal feminist." But I didn't have to strike up anything because the conversation came to me.

The owner of our new doggy friend was a woman who was a bit rough around the edges. The moment she sat down she looked at both of us for about a minute. We're used to this—it's actually kind of funny. She looked at David, then over at me, then back to David, and back at me. She did this so many times I'm surprised she didn't get vertigo.

It's hilarious to watch different personality types handle the fact they're sitting between twins. Introverts usually look at us from the corners of their eyes, trying with all their might not to turn and look fully at us. I know they want to ask the question, but they're not willing to put themselves out there to do it.

David, always the extrovert, typically just comes out and says it, "Yes, we're twins," and then he goes right back to typing on his computer.

This woman, however, was the opposite of introverted. She was the opposite of anyone we had encountered in a long time. After seven or eight revolutions of staring at us she blurted out, "So are ya'll twins or what?"

I love people like this who say exactly what they're thinking at all times with no filters. I mean, sometimes it's rough when you have to pick up the pieces of your fractured ego when they touch that small part of your soul housing all your insecurities. But at least you know they're not hiding anything toward you. I'd much rather have someone tell me they can't stand me than to be nice to my face and harbor bitterness for some unknown offense. Isn't honesty and openness the essence of a good relationship anyway?

I digress.

David, never shy of speaking up even though it's "my turn," responded, "Our dad has two wives—he was with the ugly one."

She belly-laughed. I knew then that I was going to enjoy this conversation despite the dog's butt now fully placed on my right leg.

She was my assignment. The dog was my distraction. The question was, on which would I focus?

It's funny how God sets us up moments like this, where the very thing He wants us to do is surrounded by so many distractions. I think He does it because of the power of choice. Without choice, there can be no true love.

I could be distracted by the dog or her abrupt personality, or I could go all in and stand in the gap. And this time, armed with the memory of when I chose to be distracted by my own desire for comfort, I fully locked in to complete my assignment.

For the first thirty minutes, she vented about everything bad in her life, starting with her boss. After hearing how she described the guy, I was ready to fight him if I saw him. I knew she just needed to get some of her frustration out, so I let her unleash the fury in her heart until she was completely out of steam.

In the course of that half-hour, I was listening as best I could, not just with my head to understand what she was saying, but also with my heart to comprehend what she was feeling. I've discovered this to be a good bridge-building quality.

When we talk with people, we need to constantly look for what's broken or bruised and seek to connect them to the God who brings healing and who can breathe life into what's dead.

As she talked, I started to see a few things emerge—a couple fractured relationships, bitterness from a past hurt, and a fear of being alone. Another revelation! This is why she needed the dog. During our little talk, she told me she was a single mother who traveled so much for her job she needed the dog to keep her company.

There was my opening. She felt alone. I let her continue talking while I tucked this thought away until I had a chance to let her know she was definitely *not* alone.

Come to find out, she was brought up in church, but she wasn't interested in all the "churchy" stuff anymore. I can't really blame her.

Religion has a way of burning people out pretty fast. But relationship—now that's something that can light your fire forever.

What I knew about this woman was she had a relationship problem. So, I went right in and shared with her everything I know about having a relationship with God and being in community with others.

She was intrigued, but I could tell I wasn't getting through. As I continued to talk, I realized that even though I recognized exactly what her problem was, because I listened with my heart, my response was coming straight from my head. There wasn't a connection.

Fortunately, the flight attendant interrupted and asked if we wanted anything to drink. I took the time to ask the Lord to give me a word for her. He dropped a verse on me right then. Because I only knew a part of the verse, I asked my assistant, David, who was sitting on the other side of her.

"Dude, which verse has this phrase in it …," I asked.

He pulled out his Bible and flipped right to the verse. He's always been better at recall than I am. It's something I've learned to accept. God gave him that ability so he can be, well, my assistant.

The interesting thing is, as I write this, neither David nor I can remember which verse it was. I do know it had something to do with God.

The minute David read it, she got really quiet. She looked straight ahead and didn't move a muscle. I even think the weenie dog might have stopped thumping his tail on my leg.

Her lip began to quiver, and then tears began rolling down her face. The Holy Spirit prompted me. "God is chasing you," I said in a quiet voice so the people behind us couldn't hear. "He is pursuing you. You've been running, but He's telling you, 'it's time to stop running.'"

That was it. She began to cry.

After she composed herself, she looked over at me and said, "Thank you. I really needed to hear that."

I explained to her it had nothing to do with me—I was just the person God chose to bridge the gap.

We finished the rest of the plane ride talking about little things—mostly what she did at work. The plane landed, we shook hands, I gave her my contact information, and off she went with her tail-thumping, hair-shedding weenie dog.

A week later I got an email. "I was honestly not expecting to have a conversation like we had on that plane," it read. "But I just wanted to thank you for the time you took to share with me. I know I've been disconnected from God, but I've now recommitted my life to Him, and I'm going to start reading my Bible every day. I just thought I'd reach out and let you know. Thank you very much for sharing what you shared."

Only God. She experienced her miracle that day, not by any clever strategy of my own, but by the power of God's Word deposited into her heart through my mouth. She boarded that plane with a disconnect in her life, and God used me (and my assistant) to reconnect her back to Him. I'm just thankful I didn't fall asleep again.

# CHAPTER 4

# LIFE ON THE FARM

Most people know us as baseball players, or business guys, or "almost" reality TV hosts. But what you may not know is we have farming in our blood.

Our granddad on our mom's side, PaPa, was a tree farmer who had about 500 acres in Midville, Georgia. His farm was twenty miles from the nearest town, and there wasn't a Walmart in sight. We'd visit the farm every July when we were kids just so we could enjoy the gnats, poison ivy, and mosquitoes.

Oh, and the humidity! We're sweating just thinking about those summer days. Not to mention the smell. A couple hundred yards down the road from PaPa's tree farm was a pig farm. Just put yourself in a steaming hot porta-potty in the middle of July at an outdoor concert, and you'll catch our drift.

Our only respite from the heat was a cast iron bathtub out behind the house. Our mom, God rest her precious soul, put us in these tight speedo-like swim trunks and let us swim in it. We looked like a couple toolboxes in that tub, but at least we didn't die from heat exhaustion.

Despite the constant barrage of bug repellant, our mom sprayed on every inch of our bodies, the heat, and the smell from the pig farm down the road, we actually loved that old farm. Maybe it was because PaPa paid us each five cents to pick up acorns. We'd take our nickels and run to Scott's Store—a small gas station down on the corner—and buy some hard-earned candy. Sometimes PaPa even let us drive his old brown truck from the house to Scott's.

## FARM HANDS

Most days, PaPa put us to work. I (Jason) remember one time chopping tree limbs with a small ax. David and I stayed out in the woods most of the day whacking away at everything in sight. I found one small tree coming up out of the ground and took a massive swing at it, only to miss in epic proportion. Unfortunately for David, who was idiotically standing behind me, I nailed him right in the leg. It's a good thing the blade was as dull as his IQ, because he only ended up with a massive knot on his shin. You should have seen him hop up and down and scream at the top of his lungs.

Anyhow, we also loved that farm because we got a chance to see big farm equipment in action. That was a nice change for a couple city boys. PaPa had several friends nearby who grew soybeans and corn. Those guys used big tractors to pull tillers, plows, sprayers, and whatever else they could hitch to them. We still remember visiting some of those old farmers. One man had six fingers on his right hand. Once we got done staring at his hand, we mustered up the courage to ask him about his equipment.

We learned quickly that each one of the pieces of equipment had a different function. The tiller broke up the ground. The plow created deep trenches to plant the seeds. The sprayer watered and fertilized the ground. The trailer hauled produce and equipment. The thresher separated the grains from the straw. The reaper cut the crops. And the tractor is what gave them all the power to do the job they were designed to do.

You'd think we were regular farm hands knowing all that stuff, right?

These farmers let us know every one of those pieces of machinery was necessary to produce a crop. But none of it would be possible if they weren't first hitched to the tractor. And the thing that connected everything to the tractor was a simple pin—a small hitch pin created to fill a gap for one purpose alone: to connect two things so the work in the field could get done.

We'd watch these old farmers back their tractors up to their plows, aligning the hitch on the back of the tractor with the hitch on the front of the plow until the holes in both were in perfect alignment. Then they'd drop a pin in the gap. Some of the bigger tractors required three hitch pins. Once the pins were inserted, the connection was made, and the farmer could get to work. Drive off without your hitch pin in place, and nothing got done in the field that day.

We learned the value of a hitch pin on the farm when we were boys. At the same time back home, we learned the value of another type of pin.

## OPEN FOR BUSINESS

When we weren't at the farm in the summer, we were at home running a small start-up company called *Benham Brothers Lawn Mowing.* Oh yeah. Armed with a beat-up orange lawnmower and a gas can, we walked our neighborhood with pride, looking for just the right person willing to hire a couple hungry twelve-year-old boys.

Cecil Ingram was our first customer. We landed his account for $12 a cut—six bucks a piece. What a nice man he was. It feels like yesterday we were walking away from his lawn wondering why his grass looked so uneven. Apparently, you're supposed to make sure all the wheels are set at the same level before you start mowing. Live and learn. But Mr. Ingram never said a word. He just paid us with a big smile on his face.

In time, our lawn mowing company turned into a neighborhood lawn mowing dynasty, when our one client increased to five in short order. But this was more than our little mower could handle. One day the wheel started wobbling, and we had to take it off to fix it. To our surprise, we discovered the same type of pin that held a tractor and plow together was the very thing connecting the wheel to our lawnmower. Only this one was much smaller and was called a linchpin. Without this little sucker, the wheel would fall right off.

A linchpin is much the same as a hitch pin—if it's not filling the gap it was designed to fill, disconnection was the result. Without that pin, our lawn mowing business suddenly came to screeching halt until we re-secured the wheel to the axel with the linchpin.

We discovered we could buy a bag of those bad boys at the store for just a few bucks. The same was true for hitch pins. What seemed so small and insignificant by themselves quickly became strong and indispensable the moment they were placed in the gap for which they were designed.

God does the same with us. He slides us into place as a strong and indispensable link to connect heaven to earth in peoples' lives. And when we faithfully fill the gap, God's work gets done. It's an awesome reality in which we get to take part!

## LIVING A HITCH PIN LIFE

It's amazing to think a perfect God would use imperfect people to accomplish His perfect will on the earth. But that's exactly what He does, as He draws people through others—He connects the gap through us, like a hitch pin. It's one of the scariest, yet most exhilarating thoughts about God's ways!

It reminds us of the story of Moses when God chose to do a great work in the world through him.

Here was Moses, a shepherd on the backside of a mountain for more than forty years, while his people, the Israelites, were slaves in Egypt. Yet God finally heard their consistent cries for deliverance and was about to answer their prayers in a big way.

Then came the burning bush. Moses sees this thing while tending his sheep, and out from the flames he hears the Lord's voice, "I have surely seen the oppression of My people who are in Egypt, and have heard their cry … so I have come down to deliver them out of the hand of the Egyptians, and to bring them up from that land to a good and large land …" (Exodus 3:7–8).

Now put yourself in Moses's shoes (well, God actually told him to take his shoes off, but let's imagine what it was like to be him). Forty years before this, he tried using his own strength to deliver God's people out of slavery (when he killed an Egyptian), and he failed miserably. Things were not yet aligned. Now the Lord shows up all these years later and says *He's* ready to do it.

I can just imagine Moses thinking to himself, "Yes Lord! This is what I've been waiting for! Now go get 'em! Let me know how it goes."

Buuuut, that's not how it worked out. God then dropped this on him, "Come now, therefore, and I will send *you* to Pharaoh that *you* may bring My people, the children of Israel, out of Egypt" (verse 10, emphasis added).

Can you hear Moses now? "Okay, wait a second, Lord. You just said *You* were going to deliver them, and now You're telling me *I* am going to do it? What's up with that?!"

He was already concerned about his ability to speak, so it's no wonder he responded to the Lord, "Who am I that I should go to Pharaoh?" (verse 11).

Can you sense the bewilderment in his words?

Yet here's the most powerful part of the entire exchange—God replied to Moses, "... Certainly I will be with you" (verse 12).

And that's it. The Lord was going to do the work, but He wanted to do it *through* Moses.

A short time later, the Israelites were out of Egypt, no longer slaves but a free people—all because one man stood in the gap.

Although for Moses, it was a terrifying and exhilarating journey along the way, and his story shows us what happens when one person lets God use him to stand in the gap to get His work done.

And it doesn't stop there. The work of standing in the gap is a continual process, as the rest of Moses's story reveals. During his journey, the Israelites cast off the Lord's ways for their own selfish desires and created an idol. Their disconnection from God became so wide He was going to "unhitch" from them forever. Yet Moses stood in the gap once again and saved the day:

> Therefore (God) said that He would destroy them, had not Moses His chosen one **stood before Him in the gap**, to turn away His wrath, lest He destroy them. (Psalms 106:20–23, emphasis added)

Moses heeded the call—he stood in the gap (multiple times)—and brought the connection.

He wasn't the only one either because all throughout Scripture God used countless men and women to do the same thing. Esther stood before the king (Esther 5:2). Ananias taught Saul (Acts 9:6). Nathan rebuked David (2 Sam 12:7). Peter preached Pentecost (Acts 2:14). And on and on—God used people over and over again to get His work on earth done through them. The question isn't **if** He's going to do it again, it's **who** He will use to do it! When we choose to follow Jesus, we have volunteered for the job—it's who we are. We just have to hold firm to that identity, and He'll make it happen when everything is aligned.

# CHAPTER 5

# IDENTITY CRISIS

I dentity theft is at an all-time high. At the time of this writing, nearly sixty million Americans have been affected by identity theft with $16.8 billion in losses (https://www.iii.org/fact-statistic/facts-statistics-identity-theft-and-cybercrime). About the same time, we got a notice that the social security number of one of our wives had been stolen. What a helpless feeling.

But the worst possible identity theft is not when someone steals your social security number or your financial information—it's when Satan robs you of your identity in Christ. He knows very well, if he can convince you to believe you're *not* part of God's plan to do His work on the earth, he can render you powerless. Because what you think determines how you act (Proverbs 23:7 KJV).

We've all felt it. That sense of fading energy and loss of power when we lose sight of our identity in Christ. Maybe you've experienced it as confusion or lack of direction. One thing's for sure: The most empowering truth is that we are children of God, called for a purpose. This truth gives energy and conviction to even the mildest and most humble believer.

If we want to be used by God to help others connect with Him, we must hold fast to our identity in Christ. Don't let it be stolen. Our identity as ministers of God on mission as "hitch-pins" in His work must be firmly rooted in our minds.

## ANSWER THE QUESTION

In February 2014, we found ourselves on the set of *Fox & Friends* in New York city being interviewed for our first book, *Whatever The Cost*. We were talking about the importance of standing strong for your faith when one of the hosts asked, "Do you guys have any interest in being pastors or preachers going forward?"

I (Jason) responded because I knew David didn't have a clue what to say. It was my turn to answer. We have this secret code for our interviews too: He answers the first question (because he's older and he can't keep his mouth shut), and then we go back and forth the rest of the time. That way we don't talk over each other.

Every now and then "the code" bites us in the rear. David's personality is more of a proclaimer and fighter, so he likes to talk about culture and politics. I'm more of an encourager and inspirer, so I like to talk about relationships and Christian living. If the interviewer comes hard at us in a combative tone, David's inner warrior jumps for joy. I get a gut ache.

David loves the hot seat when the interviewer is trying to push us in a corner—he comes alive in those moments (okay, so I will admit, as difficult as it is to say, there are few better at handling the hot seat like he does). I hate those moments. I want the La-Z-Boy couch interview where we're all on the same team and laughing hysterically together. (David: Trust me, I like those better too).

I'll get back to my *Fox & Friends* response in a minute, but at that moment, I had the benefit of remembering our first interview on the *Megyn Kelly Show* when she asked David the first question. It was an absolute softball—the easy kind anyone could knock out of the park. I sat there thinking, "Why in the heck didn't I go first this time?" I had no clue what she was going to ask next, but I knew I would have to take it. Because it was only a four-minute segment, I had a feeling she was going to pick up the pace and throw a doozy.

When she asked the next question, I felt my face get hot. It slowly moved into my chest and then my gut. I don't remember the specific question, I just remember thinking, "This is so in David's lane." I felt David's leg shaking nervously next to mine. I knew what he was thinking, "Jason's going to strike out so bad!"

I had no idea what I was going to say. NO CLUE! A fleeting thought of "I hate our little code" crossed my mind. But although it was a perfect question for David, it was God's assignment for me. I really believe it was to show me how the Holy Spirit gives you what to say in moments like these.

I said a quick "God help me" prayer and then started talking. I have no idea what came out of my mouth after that. I just remember thinking, "Man, that sounded pretty good."

Don't worry, I'm not being prideful—I knew it wasn't me. David knew it too. After the interview, he said, "I knew you hated that question. Thank God He gave you something to say because you could have really bombed on that one."

God will always give you the words to say right when you need to say them if you're simply willing to open your mouth.

## THE NOT-SO-HOT SEAT

Now back to the set of *Fox & Friends* and the question posed to us— "Do you guys have any interest in being pastors or preachers going forward?" That question was right up my alley. Fortunately for me, it was my turn to answer. When the host asked the question, I instantly felt the Holy Spirit nudge me in the direction of identity.

"There's a false dichotomy today that says guys like us in business are not ministers," I responded as the host panel listened intently. "We don't believe that. The minute you give your heart to Christ He puts you on mission to bring Him glory. Whether you're running a talk show or preaching behind a pulpit, you are a minister, so just go out there and bring God glory."

When I was talking, I felt an energy come over me, like the Holy Spirit talking directly through me to the people watching—because identity is near and dear to the heart of God as the Bible talks about again and again.

I continued, "The devil knows how you see yourself determines how you behave. So, if he can get you thinking you're not a minister, you won't act like it. So that's our encouragement for Christians today—you *are* ministers, even if you're just wiping rear-ends at home as a stay-at-home-mom."

I said that last part in an effort to help believers understand that what determines the minister is not where you're placed or how you're paid (like a pastor at a church)—but the presence of God in your life. If you love the Lord, you are His minister on mission to bring Him glory wherever He's placed you. And God will use you. I thought of my wife who was at home with our four kids while I was in New York on the show— she's the best minister I know in one of the most undervalued ministries of all.

David topped it off with, "So the answer is yes, we will go into ministry. We're in it right now."

They got it. The light bulb turned on in their minds. As a matter of fact, one of the hosts, Elizabeth Hasselback, finished the segment with, "I've got some rear-ends to attend to at home myself!"

## WHO TOLD YOU THAT?

We struggled with our own identities back when we started our business in real estate. For years, we felt guilty for not going into "full-time ministry." Those are scare quotes, by the way.

In 2003, a few years out of professional baseball, we felt certain God wanted us to be "ministers" and go into "the ministry." We even started a website called Benham Brothers Ministries and wrote a support letter. But God told us not to go that direction and to simply start working. We were dumbfounded and confused. Why would God want us to be businessmen instead of ministers?

We didn't know exactly what to do, but because we earned our real estate licenses the year before we thought we'd try to sell a few houses to provide for our families. In professional baseball, we were minor league guys, so money wasn't growing on trees for us.

Seven years later, we had 100 real estate offices in thirty-five states with hundreds of agents, employees, and franchisees. It was totally a God thing because we built our business from the principles of the Bible. We had no idea what we were doing, and we had no business training at all. One day soon, we'll write a book about that journey.

It was during this time God revealed to us the importance of identity in Him. Each year, we held a conference and invited all our affiliates to fly in for a few days of training. During the events, we developed our leaders and taught business principles directly from the Bible, doing everything we could to help them succeed in business. The whole time, though, we felt the continued sting of guilt for building a business and not a ministry.

It was in the middle of one of those events while standing at the podium in front of a packed room of business leaders, when God clearly spoke to us. We were standing up there with our Bibles open, teaching principles of business when I (Jason) heard God ask, "Who told you that you weren't in ministry?" It was just a faint whisper, but I could hear it in my spirit.

After the event was over, I told David about it, and for the next few days, as we prayed, God spoke to us. In the same way God asked Adam in the Garden—when he was hiding from the Lord because he fell prey to Satan's lie—"Who told you that you were naked?"—God was getting to the bottom of our identity issue by first exposing the liar.

"Who told you that you weren't in ministry?" We heard that question over and over for the entire week after our conference.

For us, this question was a watershed moment. We realized Satan wanted nothing more than for us to simply think we were just real estate guys, like little hitch pins left in a bag with no purpose. But if we saw ourselves as ministers of God and on mission for Him, Satan was in trouble. We were deceived all along into thinking full-time ministry meant you had to be placed either in a church or overseas and you're paid by a nonprofit organization.

At that moment, we realized we'd been in ministry the whole time, whether we knew it or not. From this new revelation, God gave us three powerful truths that apply to every person who has accepted Christ as Savior:

- *You're a minster right where you are*—plumber, politician, parent, or pastor—it doesn't matter where you're placed or how you're paid.
- *Your mission is to bring God glory*—by being excellent at what you do wherever He has placed you.
- *Your work is worship*—our one role is to worship God through the work we do.

From that day, everything we did in business was different. We felt freedom like we'd never experienced before. We pursued our work with a newfound vigor, recognizing that worship isn't just something we do when we sing at church on Sunday morning; it's what we do at the office on Monday afternoon too. Worship, simply put, is our attempt to make God smile. We worship Him when we clean that house, or write that paper, or wash those dishes as if He's the one who gave us the job. In whatever we do, when we live to put a smile on God's face, we are worshipping Him. And when we do, He can use us powerfully to get His work done.

Identifying these powerful truths has unlocked our identity in Christ. And on this foundation, we can more effectively stand in the gap *as minsters on mission* to help others connect with God, especially in our places of work.

## WHAT'S YOUR SECRET?

About a year after this epiphany, we were asked to sit on a panel with some of the top experts in our industry. There was a large gathering of people in the audience all waiting to hear how we built our businesses and the best practices they could incorporate to build their own. At that point, our reputation had grown significantly because we were featured in several magazine and newspaper articles, including in the *Wall Street Journal*.

The first question was, "What's one thing you do that makes your business successful?"

I (Jason) was seated at the end of the row, so I would have to answer last. One by one, as each panelist gave his or her answer, I sat in my chair debating what I would say. On the one hand, I wanted to take the opportunity to point people to the Lord. But on the other, I didn't want to look like an idiot.

For about ten minutes, this debate went on in my mind, like a tug of war. "Don't look like an idiot"— "Stand strong for the Lord"—"They don't want to hear about God"—"They need to hear about Jesus …" You'd think by this point in my walk with Jesus I'd boldly say what needed to be said in confidence without any fear, but that wasn't the case. It's still a struggle for me.

By the time the person next to me was speaking, my heart was in a full-on footrace. That old familiar hot feeling in my chest came back as I took a few deep breaths to calm my nerves. It's funny how this works, but this nervous feeling is typically God's way of saying, "Go ahead and stand for Me." It feels that way every time.

When it came to me, I took the microphone and said, "I just have to be honest and tell you the number one secret to our success—it's God Almighty." I saw blank faces—people just staring back up at me as if to say, "Really? That's all you got?"

I continued, "We've made a commitment to get on our knees every morning in our office and pray for the success of our company as well as the wellbeing of our employees. We first pray like it all depends on God, and then we work like it all depends on us. We do a lot of other things as well, but if you want to know the primary key to our success—this is it."

Most of the people in the audience just sat there with no emotional response whatsoever. It's funny because I was kind of expecting the crowd to erupt in applause and carry me out on their shoulders chanting my name. I mean, I just overcame my fear—I thought for sure God would reward that with an epic ending.

When the event was over, three or four people came up to me afterward. One by one, they told me how appreciative they were that I gave God the credit and how it inspired them to be more outward in their faith. Of course, I let them know I was scared and had to rely on God to give me the strength to say it. But I knew the Lord called me there as a minister, not just a businessman.

Knowing your identity as a minister of God, regardless of where you are placed or how you are paid, is key to standing in the gap. For me, God placed me in a position to fill a specific gap at a specific time for specific people. Had I not recognized my identity as a minister at that moment, I don't think I would have responded the way I did.

That is the power of identity and the reason Satan wants to rob you of it. Don't let him. You are a minister right where you are. It doesn't matter your profession—you are to be on mission for God and to be that indispensable link between heaven and earth in the work you do. Now, make your work worship and stand in that gap!

# CHAPTER 6

# THE TIPPING POINT

K nowing who we are in Christ and heeding His call to stand in the gap fills us with energy to live out our faith in tangible ways. Fortunately for us, we had great role models who lived it out every single day as we grew up.

Our dad used to say, "If you can't tip well, don't go out to eat." Even though our family didn't have much money growing up, if we ever went out to eat, our dad lived by this motto, sometimes blowing people away with big tips.

He learned it from his dad, our grandpa, Jimmy Benham. On our birthday each year, Grandpa would take us to a nice restaurant or the local Elk's Lodge and spoil us rotten with anything we wanted to order. It was so fun. Typically, he'd sit at the bar for the first twenty minutes and buy a round for everyone seated there. It didn't matter whether he knew the people or not—if Jimmy Benham was in the room, he was the one picking up the tab.

All the servers and bartenders loved Grandpa. You'd love him too if your livelihood depended on the generosity of people like him giving good tips. His giving spilled over into every facet of his life—he was always looking to take care of people. It was just put on display when we went out to eat.

## THE GRANDPA GRID

Turns out you can tell a lot about a person by how they act when they're out to eat. In our opinion, the way we treat our servers, how willing we are to pick up the tab (if we're with others), and how well we tip reveal a lot about the type of people we are. Grandpa always topped the charts in these three areas. And as for the tip, he and Dad taught us we tip well based on not the service we receive but the people we are. Because you never know what's going on in that server's life.

This little, three-fold "Grandpa-Grid" actually helped us filter out those we wanted to do business with from those we didn't early in our career. Even if someone had the expertise we needed for a job or possessed raving reviews from past clients, if we went to lunch or dinner and they failed in these three areas, it put a sour taste in our mouths.

When we were younger, we had a baseball coach who typically got the first two right—he was always friendly with the servers and he usually picked up the tab—but when it came to leaving a good tip, you may as well have asked him to bench press the buffet bar. It just wasn't happening.

Sometimes our team would amass a several-hundred-dollar check our coach would pay—then leave a $20 tip. We all knew of his tipping struggle. But our assistant coach always remedied the situation. He'd wait until we all got on the bus, walk over to where the check lay on the table, and slap down enough cash to make the servers happy—really happy.

Our coach was a good man, honestly, but this tipping thing showed a weak link in his armor. Heck, we're still talking about it all these years later.

What we've discovered is there are few better ways to connect with people than at a local restaurant. It's a fantastic place to establish relationships with those we may see over and over. And when we treat them well by tipping well, it often opens a door to their hearts.

*Treat 'em well and tip 'em well.* That has a nice ring to it.

## CHECK, PLEASE

When Tori and my [Jason's] kids were young, holding down the fort for her while I was at the office was as exhausting as working the graveyard shift after running a marathon. So, Friday night date night became the one thing that helped pull her through the week. I'm sure you moms reading this have been there before. Now that our kids are older, we've finally got a little more breathing room, but in those days, Friday nights were sacred.

One Friday night, we decided to eat at a nice Chinese chain restaurant about fifteen minutes from our house. Their lettuce wraps were off the charts—we craved those bad boys like a fish craves water.

This particular night we got into a good conversation with our server, which was actually odd for us at the time. When you've got three kids below the age of four years at home, eating out might be the only time you can talk without interruption. So, we took advantage of every minute we got alone.

This night was different. After our server broke our hearts by telling us the devastating news they no longer carried the dessert we loved, he began telling us about his personal life. We learned he was divorced, had a daughter, was a student at a local college, and was actively seeking to reconnect with God. That last part we pulled out of him—then the conversation went deep fast.

At the end of our meal, we both felt a prick in our hearts to bless this guy through our tip. We wanted it to be big enough to thank him for his service and make an impact on his life at the same time. We agreed on a number, paid the bill, left the tip, wrote a little "Jesus Loves You" on the receipt, and walked out.

As we walked to our car we heard someone coming behind us. When we turned around, we saw our server running toward us. He ran up to us and wrapped his arms around us. "You guys have no idea how much this means to me," he said breathing heavily from his run. "I can't believe you just did that. I needed it so bad."

"Dude, God has blessed us, and we want to bless you," I said. "He's got a plan for you and your daughter, and He just wanted you to know He loves you. He simply used us to tell you that."

After another few hugs and several more handshakes, he went back inside.

Two months later, on another Friday night, Tori was craving seafood. I think the gift card in her purse was the source of her craving.

When we sat down, our server walked up, and low and behold, it was the same guy as before. We looked at each other in disbelief. He was as shocked to see us as we were to see him.

"Man, this is crazy," he said. "I didn't think I'd ever see you guys again. I still think about what you did for me. Thank you so much."

"No prob …" I started.

"I don't want you guys to think you have to do that again or anything," he said. "It's all good. I'm working two jobs now so all is well."

We asked him about his daughter and his school and his faith. He was doing much better in every category, especially his faith. "I've actually read passages in the Bible a couple times," he told us. "And I'm going to get back into church."

"Good for you," I responded. "Now how about that baked cod?" Tori is a sucker for flaky white fish.

After polishing off our food, we started prepping for our traditional after-dinner rendezvous at our favorite, local ice cream shop just a few doors down. It has the absolute best combination of ice cream shop/chocolate factory/fudge maker all crammed into one. The minute you open the door you're blanketed in rich chocolate aromas combined with fresh waffle cones and candied apples. My go-to is a mountain of chocolate chip ice cream in a waffle cone with a few dark chocolate peanut clusters thrown in for good measure. Tori typically gets the maple walnut ice cream in a cup and orders a waffle cone separately. Who does that? Put the ice cream in the cone, girl! She says the cone tastes better on its own. I say she's nuts—the cone was made for the ice cream.

Anyway, after our server-friend brought us the check, Tori and I felt that same familiar nudge and knew right away God wanted us to do it again. So that's what we did—same amount, same message.

Before we could even get ten feet away from the restaurant, he busted out the front door and threw his hands up, "You did it again!" This time he was almost in tears and couldn't stop hugging us.

"Why did you do that?" he asked.

"Bro, God is loving you through us," I said. "We're nobody special—just two Christians who want you to experience the same love from God we do. Jesus loves you and has a plan for you."

"That's awesome, man," he said. "I really feel like God is trying to get to me."

With that he walked back inside, shaking his head in disbelief, while Tori and I made our way to Kilwins. Our ice cream tasted extraordinarily good that night.

God wants to connect with people all around us, so in everything we do, it's important to keep our eyes up and ears open to see what God would have us do. We've found one of the simplest ways to connect heaven to earth for those God brings into our path is to simply tip well with a little "Jesus loves you!" on the tab. Who knows, that just might be the right word at the right moment God uses to satisfy a hungry soul.

# CHAPTER 7

# MIND THE GAP

Have you ever traveled the underground tube system in London? It's a pretty cool experience, especially when you do it with your whole family as I (Jason) did while writing this book. Let me start by apologizing to all Americans, as we quickly became "that" family. You know, the one that defines the typical American tourist the locals wish would vacation elsewhere. I think it had something to do with my youngest daughter hanging from the train car handrail upside down—or something like that.

Riding the tube immersed us into English culture as we crammed into the train with hundreds of Londoners on their way to work, the store, or wherever their busy schedules were taking them—all adhering to the seemingly unwritten rule, "no talking."

Nobody said a word. There may have been a quiet conversation somewhere, but for the most part, people were buried in their phones, reading a book, or staring out the window. But then, as we arrived at each station, the doors would snap open like clockwork and a voice over the intercom would break the silence—"Mind the gap!" Sometimes it was the voice of a man; other times it was that of a woman. But every time it was with a deep, British accent. It sounded more like, "Mind the gop!"

Every stop. Every time. It was the same phrase, over and over. "Mind the gap!" The fine folks who govern the city of London care so much about their people's safety they remind them consistently and repetitively about this gap.

It was a simple statement that revealed a singular truth—there was a gap between the train and the platform, a disconnect to which travelers must pay close attention. Refuse to show concern for the gap, and you could get hurt.

It made me think about this book and the reality of the spiritual gap David and I are writing about—that disconnect between God and people, His truth and our ways, as we journey through life. And the first step toward standing in this gap is to be mindful of it—"mind the gap."

In London, the doors on the train didn't slowly open and close—they were more like giant spring-loaded calipers shooting open and closed with force, ready to grab your leg at any moment and drag you down the tunnel. This made traveling with a family of six quite the experience. Tori's greatest fear was that five of us would make it off leaving left on the train—most likely Lundi, our youngest.

Fortunately, we never got separated, but we did have one close call. We were getting off the train and our youngest son was moving too slowly. The train pulled to a stop, the doors shot open as "Mind the gap" came over the intercom. We hurriedly got off the train and stood on the platform, only to realize Jake was still inside, lugging his suitcase toward the door. Then a voice came over the intercom, "Stand clear of the door, this train is departing."

What does a dad do in that situation? There was no phone booth close by, so I couldn't change into my red cape. I did what any other dad would do—I jumped over the gap and straddled it, putting my back to the door. With one foot on the platform and the other in the train, I stood there in an "I dare you to take off with my son" pose until Jake finally was able to get off the train. He made it safely across the gap, but not without me taking a door-smack in the back a few times.

At that moment, I stood in the gap for my son. There was no way he was going to make it to the other side without me stepping in, and I was not going to budge until I knew he was safe. Jake was spared from taking a tube ride all by his lonesome because someone stood in the gap for him (please, hold your applause).

In the same way, God wants us to stand in the gap for others. It's not enough for us to simply "mind the gap" (or recognize it)—we must be willing to stand in the gap as God leads, even when it hurts. Of course, God could handle this all on His own, but He doesn't do it that way. He uses you and me to do the job. He uses us to stand in the gap so our fellow travelers in life can make it safely to the other side.

## WITNESS

For those of us who follow Christ, there is no greater way to stand in the gap for others than to share our faith. Jesus charged us with this mission in Matthew 28:16–20. He didn't say, "Go live well, and folks will find me on their own." He could have just dropped Gospel bombs on people out of heaven, but that's not the way it works. He chose us to share the good news to get the work done. It's what Paul told young Timothy to do as he went about his daily life—"do the work of an evangelist," (2 Timothy 4:5), which might be translated, "tell people the good news about Jesus."

We're thankful our dad showed us how to do this early on.

## TESTIMONY AT TEXACO

"Boys, hop in the car!" Dad said, "We need some gas." For two young boys, gas stations held perpetual promise. For us, they were like a dazzling oasis in the dessert—aisles of candy and convenience food, all in an air-conditioned store bringing relief from the Texas heat. But our dad rarely bought us candy bars or Cokes when he lugged us along for the weekly fill up. What he had in mind was telling people about Jesus.

It's convicting when we think back to those times as young boys. It was like clockwork. Dad would step out of the car to the gas pump and begin talking to the person on the other side.

"What's your name?" we heard him ask while we hid inside the car, peeking out the window so we wouldn't be spotted by any of our fifth-grade classmates.

After the exchange of names, Dad would say, "Do you mind if I ask you a question?"

"Uh, okay," was the typical response. They weren't sure if he was some freak or a genuinely nice guy.

"If you were to die ten seconds from now, where would you go?"

What a way to start off a conversation.

If they responded, "I don't know," then he'd tell them about Jesus. If they said, "Heaven," he'd say, "Alright then. If God were to say, 'Why should I let you into My Heaven?' how would you answer?"

At that point, the ice was broken. A conversation between the two motorists began as we kids sat in the car melting in the Texas heat. A car fills with gas pretty quickly, so those little talks never lasted long—just long enough for the person to feel encouraged and maybe learn about the path to eternal life.

## LIFESTYLE EVANGELISM

Whether we liked Dad's method or not, He could always be counted on to share his faith. He took Christ's final words seriously, especially the part where He told us to make disciples of all nations. Believers know it as the Great Commission. But unfortunately, it's become more of an omission in our lives. Often, we meet folks and maybe even spend years knowing them without ever sharing the good news of Jesus Christ.

Since we were those young and embarrassed kids just hoping our dad would leave strangers alone and buy us some junk food and a Coke at the gas station, we heard about what's been called "lifestyle evangelism." This is a term coined to do evangelism another way. The idea is to attract others to our faith through intentional living. And, of course, it's important we live out our faith. After all, Jesus called his disciples "a city on a hill" because folks notice when we radiate God's light. But living for God without sharing His truth is selfishness. Living must lead to telling.

Fact is, telling people even good news can be challenging. Just the other day, I (David) realized I had known a guy for almost ten years, and I never once told him about Jesus. Not once. And he's a close friend.

Sure, I've lived in a manner he respects, but I've never even attempted to tell him about the hope I have in Christ. Talk about needing to stand in the gap.

As I searched my heart to find out why, I discovered I was more concerned about our relationship than his soul. I didn't want to talk about something that might offend him or push him away from me. So, I've avoided the topic. This is *no bueno*.

We often put more weight on the risk than the reward when it comes to sharing our faith. We think more about the risk of looking like a fool than we do the reward of connecting a person to God.

Talking about Jesus takes courage. It's easy to say, "God bless you" to the bank teller at the drive-through window just before driving away. That's a good habit. But it's another thing to tell someone about Jesus when the opportunity presents itself. It requires us to get rid of all self-consciousness and think in light of eternity.

## SERMON ON THE MOUND

In our book *Living Among Lions*, I (Jason) told a story about a time when an opportunity to share my faith landed right in my lap. I was in my second year of professional baseball with the Frederick Keys, the Class A team for the Baltimore Orioles.

Lots of kids attended the ballpark with their parents for "student night." The place was packed—dads holding a ballpark frank in one hand and a Coke in the other while moms balanced a family-sized popcorn in one hand and little junior in the other—covered with cotton candy.

Just before the game, as we were stretching in right field, one of the marketing assistants jogged over. She looked my way and said, "Hey Jason. The front office wants you to address the crowd for a few minutes before the game. You good with that?"

"Uh, yea I guess," I said with slight hesitation. Her request caught me off guard. I mean, we were literally ten minutes from game time. I had no clue what I should say.

Honestly, I said "yes" before I could really think about it. I think it was a knee-jerk reaction from having just memorized 1 Peter 3:15 where it says, "Always be prepared to give an answer to everyone who asks you to give the reason for the hope that you have."

*Why is that verse in the Bible?* I wondered as I began to feel slight regret for agreeing so fast.

Then she said, "Because it's student night, they want you to speak on the value of reading and studying."

*Well isn't that nice,* I thought. *I can't think of anything more exciting to speak about than that!*

Before I could respond she said, "You only have a few minutes, so make it quick. You don't have time to preach a sermon or anything."

Funny they thought I would preach just because I was a Christian. This was a few months into the season, so by that time, most everyone knew I was a believer.

Right there I had a decision to make. Stand in front of everyone and give a little popcorn speech on the value of reading books and studying—a message everyone would soon forget—or let it be known Jesus was Lord of my life—the message no one can ever forget. I knew I didn't have enough time to share the full Gospel, only about sixty seconds.

I jumped up and made my way to the clubhouse. I wanted a few minutes alone to pray before I got out there.

My pregame routine in professional baseball was to find an open bathroom stall in the clubhouse, get down on one knee, and pray. I had already prayed in the stall for this game, but I went in for another round in hopes of a little inspiration for my pre game speech.

"Lord," I said as I kneeled in that bathroom stall. "I need your help. I have no clue what to say. But I know these people need to hear about You. So please give me the words to say."

As I walked out of the clubhouse, my heart was racing. I still didn't know what to say. "God, You've got to come through for me," I whispered, slowly making my way to the field.

The crowd of 5,000 grew silent when I walked toward home plate, the pit in my stomach growing bigger and bigger the quieter it got. Even the other team got quiet as they lined their dugout waiting to hear what I would say.

I was accustomed to walking toward home plate with a bat in my hand and a job to get a hit for the team. But this was a completely different ballgame. I had a microphone in my hand and a job to deliver a message from God.

Dad always told me, "Don't let the butterflies in your stomach keep you from doing what's right. Make them fly in formation!"

As I looked over the crowd, I felt a boldness come over me. It's hard to explain unless you've experienced it yourself. But the minute I grabbed the microphone and looked at the faces of the people in the stadium—the very people I knew God had a message for—I knew exactly what God wanted to say to them.

"I've heard it said," I began. "The most important things in life are the people you meet and the books you read. Well, I'm here to tell you the best book I've ever read is the Holy Bible, and the best person I've ever met is Jesus Christ. He's changed my life, and He'll change yours too if you'll commit to studying His book."

The crowd erupted in applause. People were whistling and parents were yelling, "Way to go!" There must have been a few Christian schools there, because their reactions were as if they were saying, "Finally! Someone just said it!"

There were plenty of people who didn't clap, but at that moment, it didn't bother me. I knew I had the smile of Heaven. God not only helped me overcome my natural inhibition to share my faith publicly, but He also gave me the exact words I needed in just the right moment. I was able to talk about the value of reading and studying, which fulfilled my obligation to the front office. But I was also able to share my faith, which fulfilled my obligation to God.

After the game, I was mobbed with kids and parents. It was normal for kids to get autographs after a game, but what wasn't normal was the number of parents who thanked me for what I said. Many of them mentioned they were thrilled their kids got to see a professional athlete be vocal about his faith.

If they only knew how difficult those ten minutes were leading up to it.

Later, that same marketing assistant approached me. But before she could say anything, I said, "I didn't make anybody in the front office mad, did I? I just couldn't let that opportunity pass."

She replied, "Actually, no. Everyone loved it. Good job." (Phew. Wipe the forehead.)

God gave me an opportunity to share my faith that day, not just with my life but with my mouth. For the newer players on my team, that was the first time they heard me verbalize my faith. They saw my ways, but that night they also got to hear my words.

There have been plenty of times I failed to speak boldly for my faith. But that night became a powerful reminder of what God can do when we simply open our mouths and tell people about Jesus. You never know the lives you're affecting when you do.

## GREAT COMMISSION

We have few friends who model how to share his faith better than our buddy, Matt Brown. Talk about bold—this dude is the poster child for boldness when it comes to telling people about Jesus. When we heard his story, how he struggled with shyness since he was a kid, we were so encouraged we had to share it.

We thought you'd like to hear it in Matt's own words.

### MATT'S STORY

I was this tall, skinny—okay, scrawny—kid from Minnesota growing up in a Christian home. I accepted the Lord early in life and went to a Christian middle school, but in high school, I went to the local public school. I was the new kid dropped into an intimidating, wild, and crazy environment. I was scared for most of that first year.

But God was doing a work in my life at this point—I actually started wanting to learn more about God. As I spent time reading my Bible, I found myself wanting my classmates to learn what I was learning. So, I started a Bible study with a small group of students who were interested, but I kept it really quiet. Aside from a few personal encounters, I wasn't vocal about my faith. The self-consciousness of adolescence coupled with my natural shyness made it easy for me to sit in the background and blend in.

At the beginning of my senior year, I began to feel a deep burden for all the people in my high school who didn't yet know the Lord, but I wasn't sure how to go about reaching them.

I played each week in a worship band that had permission to play at our school, and one day we had a speaker come who invited our band to come lead worship for an outreach they held in New Orleans. I agreed to go.

## MARDI GRAS

When I told my parents I was going to Mardi Gras to play worship music, they were skeptical, wondering what they were sending me to. Mardi Gras had already gained the reputation as the biggest party scene in America, so it wasn't the typical place you'd send your teenage son!

During the first night, we went out to Bourbon Street and saw this mass of people drinking, laughing, stumbling, and making out. This introverted, Christian high schooler from Minnesota was totally out of his element. I was nervous, scared, and maybe even a little nauseated—in the middle of the largest street party in the country.

I don't know how to explain it, but the Spirit of God fell on me that night. I overcame whatever fears I had, whatever shyness I had, and I stepped out and began to share the good news of Jesus with people. It was a refreshing boldness I was unaccustomed to. It felt good. Really good. I was able to face my fears and move forward obediently as He gave me the courage to walk it out.

The first few people we approached listened for a few seconds and then walked away as they laughed at us. But I wasn't discouraged. I felt God's presence.

Looking back, I can see that it was my simple obedience despite my fear that tapped into the Holy Spirit's power. I really felt like nothing could hold me back from talking about Jesus, no matter how people responded.

After striking out several times (although there is no such thing as a strike out when it comes to witnessing), I came across a group of dudes a foot taller than me and twice my weight. They looked like they were in the NFL. "Hey, do you believe in Jesus?" I asked. No soft opening or proper introductions. I'm not advocating this for every situation; it's just what I did at that moment.

My question took them by surprise. But a few short minutes later, three of the roughest looking guys bowed their heads and accepted Jesus as their Savior. God had already aligned things in their lives for just that moment.

It was intoxicating seeing the power of the Gospel! There I was—a scrawny little kid from Minnesota in the middle of Mardis Gras—with these three total strangers as they opened their hearts to Christ. I was hooked. Right then and there, I promised to do the same when I went back to my high school.

## BACK AT HOME

It's one thing to witness to total strangers who may never see you again. But it's a different matter altogether to share Christ with your own peers who see you all day every day. I really didn't know what to do, but I knew I didn't want my own fear to hold me back. So, I prayed and fasted, asking God for direction. I went into the band room during lunch break one day and prayed on my knees, "God, how can my classmates hear about you?"

God urged me to be bold, to simply stand up and speak. But I will admit, I kept putting it off. It was this pit-in-my-stomach kind of feeling—dread and excitement all mixed into one. I knew what He was telling me to do, but there was that fear again. And I wasn't sure exactly how to do it.

I decided to go for it on the second-to-last day of high school during my senior year. I got my Bible study friends together, and we did a prayer walk around the halls of the school, asking for God's presence to show up as I was about to do something I still can't believe I did. After this prayer and before I could talk myself out of it, I made a beeline for the cafeteria.

As soon as I walked in, I went to a table and stepped up on top. I just stood up there and belted out, "Do you know that Jesus loves you? He has changed my life, and I want Him to change yours too."

All the talk in the entire cafeteria went silent. There was a reverent hush over the room.

Somehow, I talked for five straight minutes about the love of Jesus. The entire experience was surreal. It was like I watched myself speaking, in shock that it was actually me standing there delivering the message. I knew it was God speaking *through* me.

As I was talking, one of the teachers started walking toward me with a serious look on his face. He had a reputation of being the tough disciplinarian at school, so I was expecting the worst. When he got to me he said, "Stand on the chair, not the table."

You got it! No problem!

I talked for a few more minutes, and to my amazement, the entire lunchroom erupted in applause. I even think I heard a few people cheering. I thought I would meet with some resistance—maybe even some persecution, but it was the complete opposite. It was so successful, I stayed and did the same thing for the second lunch period and received the same reaction.

Sixty students came up to me in the hall outside the lunchroom for prayer after those two lunches. Sixty kids! I knew then that my calling was to be a full-time evangelist for the rest of my life. And that's what I am to this day.

The whole experience showed me the power of boldness. My heart was broken for my high school, but I couldn't stand in the gap for my fellow students until I broke out of my shyness and boldly followed the Holy Spirit's leading. What started out as a burden turned into a fruitful ministry when I chose to do something bold for the Lord.

While you may not be called to stand on a lunchroom table, you are called to stand somewhere at sometime for someone. Don't let your fear keep you from standing in the gap, being that bridge (or hitch pin) that connects them to God.

So, let's commit to doing the work Christ called us to do, whether at the gas station, the ball field, or the lunchroom. We may never know just how impactful our words might be.

# CHAPTER 8

# FAITH ON THE FIELD

B y the time Jason and I were drafted into professional baseball at twenty-two years old, we had read through the Bible four times. We made that commitment just before we graduated high school and headed to college. Little did we know just how vital it would be to the work God had in store for us.

I (David) remember reading my Bible the morning of the draft in 1998. I didn't know what round I'd be selected, but I felt pretty strongly I'd go early. After the Tigers called that morning, I figured I was headed to Detroit. But a few hours later, the Red Sox called and said they selected me in the twelfth round. It was later than I expected, but I was thankful I'd been picked. Based on the passage of Scripture I had been meditating on, I knew I had work to do.

I was thinking about Abraham and how he built an altar as a witness to God whenever he settled in a new land. He used the altar as a place to worship God and to express his affection. He wanted people to know he was a God follower.

This struck me because I was about to settle in my own new land in the minor leagues. Wherever Abe went, he made sure God went with him, in a clear and marked way. So, when the Red Sox drafted me, I felt the Lord tell me to do the same thing. I started making plans to build a large wooden altar in the middle of Fenway Park. Ha! Not really.

## WHAT WILL MY ALTAR BE?

As I asked God what my altar would look like, I felt Him lead me to set up a Bible study in each clubhouse where I was going to play. That would be my altar. And I wasn't to focus on trying to get the guys to come—I was to simply read my Bible in the clubhouse and let the guys come to me.

It took me a few days to settle into the idea. Not because I was ashamed of the Bible but because I wasn't sure how a bunch of minor league guys would respond to me reading it in front of them. I was nervous. But God gave me courage when He reminded me I was not to focus on how the guys would respond, I was simply to focus on obeying Him. Duty is ours. Results are God's. Plus, most of the players at this time just sat around playing their Nintendo Gameboys (I'm dating myself here), so why wouldn't I read the Bible instead?

My first minor league team for the Sox was with the Lowell Spinners, a small Massachusetts town just outside Boston. The stadium was brand new, and up to that point, it was the nicest stadium I'd ever played in. We sold out every night. Thousands of fans piled in each night to watch players from around the world compete—all of us with hopes of making it to the Big Leagues. I think we heard the song, "Cotton-Eyed Joe," a few hundred times that summer.

The first day I went into the clubhouse, I paused in front of my locker and prayed.

"Lord, I commit this locker, this place, these men, and this season to you," I prayed. "I ask you to give me the strength to be your hands and feet here. Oh, and while you're at it, will you please help me get to the Big Leagues?!"

I always had to throw that last line in there—and in pretty much every prayer over the four years I played in the pros.

Every time I moved to a new team throughout the minors, I prayed the same prayer. I committed each clubhouse, every team, and all the players to the Lord. Then I'd sit at my locker and open my big, green Life

Application Bible Fert bought me the year I played in Torrington. As I sat at my locker that first day in the Lowell Spinners clubhouse with my Bible open, I asked God to bring guys to me for a Bible study.

## FIRST DAY

The first day players arrive in a new town to start a season is always an experience. Guys from the University of California, Los Angeles, Louisiana State University, and Podunk High School USA to Venezuela, Cuba, and the Dominican Republic all converge in one location. Countless life experiences, each guy viewing the world through a different set of lenses, yet all aiming for the same goal.

As guys rolled into the clubhouse, a young, second-round draft pick pitcher named Mike threw his bag down next to mine. I overheard him having a conversation where he talked about the brand new 1998 silver Corvette he bought with his signing bonus. When he ended up in the locker next to mine, I knew God handed me my first assignment.

But I didn't hit him with the Gospel right then and there. I knew my play on the field, behavior off the field, and consistent Bible reading at my locker would be enough to get him asking questions. Sure enough, within a few days, my plan worked. We played the Tigers; he pitched and I caught, and they couldn't touch us. Turns out we were a pretty good combo on the field.

After the game, he sat next to me. "So ….," he said with a long pause, "are you religious or what?" And that was it—we were off to the races.

It turned out Mike had previous experience with the Lord, but he wasn't walking with Him any longer. Baseball became his number one priority, and according to him, it was paying off. But over the next few weeks, he began reading his Bible again. A few weeks after that, he rededicated his life to the Lord, and we went into full discipleship mode. Two other players eventually joined us, and I made my dorm room our Bible study spot. My altar was built.

I used batting practice as my time to walk around and get to know the guys. For ninety minutes every day, I walked from player to player talking about life, baseball, and faith. The hardest part was breaking the ice, but I realized after several weeks of being with the team I had earned their respect because I worked hard and always got to the field early. Those guys knew I meant business about baseball, so when I talked about Jesus they were willing to listen.

In time, more and more guys came to me about their life problems. It was common to get knocks on my hotel room door at 2:00 A.M. when loose living finally caught up to them. Minor league baseball was proving to be quite the missionary endeavor.

That season ended, and we all went our separate ways. In professional baseball, you don't see many of your teammates again after trades, promotions, and releases in the offseason. That's what happened with Mike and me. But years later, in a sports magazine article, I read Mike's story of how he made it to the Big Leagues just a few years into professional baseball. In the article, he mentioned a Bible study that helped him start off on the right foot his first year in the league. Heaven to earth, through an altar to God.

## NEW GUY

The next year, I was assigned to the Sarasota Red Sox in the Florida State League. Because of an injury, I arrived two months into the season, so many relationships on the team were already formed. There I was, the new guy, all nervous about making a good impression, knowing full well my assignment was to crack open my Bible.

I felt a tinge of fear because many of those players were older, better, and more experienced than I was. The temptation to just sit back and blend in was strong. But I sat by my locker, remembered my commitment, and cracked open my Bible anyway. Small victory. But the clubhouse was too small—we were all on top of each other. So, I decided to go outside to a picnic table in front of the players' entrance to read.

## PRAYER AT THE PICNIC TABLE

The first player who came up to me was a six-foot four-inch 250-pound hulk of a man named Damien. He was another top-round draft pick with tons of Red Sox money invested in him. He recently divorced and rarely got to see his young daughter. It didn't matter how much money he had or the incredible upside potential the Red Sox saw in him, he wanted to be a good dad and try to work things out with his estranged wife. I'll never forget when he walked up to the picnic table after a workout and asked me for prayer. He leaned his pine tar–laced bat against the table and plopped down right next to me. I closed my Bible, we talked for a few minutes, and I put my hand on his shoulder and prayed for him.

Over the next few weeks, Damien met me at the picnic table almost every day. As soon as batting practice was over, we'd be out there, sometimes for more than an hour, talking, reading Scripture, and praying together. I didn't know it at first, but I soon realized Damien was the leader of the team. One by one, other players began to meet us at the picnic table, too. Like clockwork, as soon as we picked up the balls from batting practice, the guys moseyed out to the picnic table and wait for me to arrive. It was like a little church gathering but with a little tobacco and occasional curse word from the congregation.

I watched as the Spirit of the Lord began softening the hearts of the guys—about five of them at that point—and a breakthrough was just right around the corner.

Damien asked if he and I could meet, just the two of us, after batting practice one day. So I met him at the picnic table. I could see the conviction of God moving in his heart as he fought back the tears.

"I really want to surrender my life to Jesus," he said. "But I don't want to give up drinking and partying with the guys. I like that stuff too much."

His humility and vulnerability were refreshing in a league full of egos.

"Bro, the fact you admitted what's holding you back is the first step," I told him. "But you can't let that keep you from going all in. God will change everything in your life and give you new desires."

He took a few deep breaths, put his head in his hands, and started bawling his eyes out. He was sobbing as he prayed out loud, "God forgive me. I want you in my life. I give you my heart. Save me from my sins."

I sat next to him quietly praying as the Holy Spirit did His work. I still remember his navy Red Sox shirt cut off just above his belt, his worn batting gloves laying on the table, and his massive baseball cleats digging in the ground as he prayed. And I had a front-row seat to see heaven fill Damien's heart for the very first time. After his prayer, he gave me a massive, insanely tight bear hug—the kind that can squeeze out a few unwanted bodily noises if you ate broccoli the night before. Then we hurried into the clubhouse for the game.

For the remainder of the season, Damien was a radically transformed man. So much so that for the next few weeks, one player after another, seeing the change in Damien's life, began joining us at the picnic table after batting practice. The next thing I knew, we had nearly twenty players on a daily basis at Bible study.

I found myself studying every morning so I'd be prepared to share God's Word in the afternoon. Knowing they would be waiting for me at the picnic table proved to be the extra accountability I needed to move from *reading* my Bible to *studying* it. I soon discovered I was mentoring guys' spiritually more than playing baseball professionally—and that's exactly why God had me there.

The Lord did something special with the guys on our team that season, and the picnic table became our altar where we worshipped Him together. It was a safe space for them where they knew they could go and meet with God. In all my years of professional baseball, I never saw anything quite like my experience in Sarasota.

I knew God was up to something special that season. So much good stuff was happening, I honestly expected at any moment I'd get called up to the Big Leagues. But with only two weeks left in the season, the team manager pulled me aside.

"Hey man," he said. "Skip needs to see you in his office."

Oh boy. What did I do? Was it my Bible study? I had no idea.

I slowly walked into our manager's office. "You wanted to see me, Skip?" I asked.

"Hey, bud. We just traded you to the St. Louis Cardinals."

Do what?! Talk about a curve ball.

Thoughts about my career and my family rushed through my head—I was in a tailspin for a few minutes. Then I thought about the Bible study. It was going so well, and I wanted to keep it going the rest of the year, but God had other plans. His altar was established, others could carry it forward, and I was moving on.

## CALLED UP

One of the first things the Cardinals did was invite me to Major League Spring Training. I would be a teammate to many guys I watched play on television for years. So, when I got there, I had to fight back the tendency to be star struck because God called me to start a Bible study with the Cards just as I did with the Red Sox. Two of the first guys in Bible study that first Spring Training were future Hall of Famer Albert Pujols and Cardinals' future Manager Mike Matheny. We met on the picnic table by the batting cages outside the clubhouse each week before we took the field.

It was an amazing time of ministry during the next few seasons I played in the Cards system. Two years and three injuries later, my time as a minister in professional baseball came to an end.

Looking back, I'm so thankful for what I learned about Abraham and his altar of worship. That became a calling for me everywhere I went in the pros. For me, it was a simple Bible study. For you it may be something completely different—like a bimonthly mommy-daughter date, helping the local soup kitchen on Thursdays, teaching art at a home-school cooperative, or even having lunch with a different coworker each day. Whatever it is, we need to recognize that connecting people to God is most often something very simple we can do in our daily routine. As I look back on my time throughout the minor leagues, I realize all I had to do was sit at my locker or picnic table, open my Bible, and wait for God to move.

# CHAPTER 9

# A PACKED LUNCH

To us, faithfulness may have looked like starting a picnic table Bible study in the Minor Leagues and sharing our faith to teammates in batting practice, but to our mom, it looked a lot more like packing a lunch.

"I'll trade you for your lunch."

We heard those six words repeated probably a thousand times in high school (well, maybe not a thousand, but a lot). The reason for this was our mom took our school lunches seriously. So seriously we rarely went to school with a packed lunch. Mom made and delivered our lunches from scratch every day. Call us spoiled or whatever you want—we don't care—because our mom knew how to show love to her hungry puppies.

From the moment our screen door slapped behind us in the morning to thirty minutes before the noon lunch bell, our mom was at home working away in our closet-sized kitchen, whipping up a lunch fit for King Solomon's table. Although she didn't have the budget of a king, she put together some of the best lunches two growing boys could ever have—all neatly packed into Tupperware containers.

When 11:30 A.M. rolled around, the hunger hounds in our teenage stomachs moved from barking to straight up howling. The minute we heard the lunch bell ring, we'd dart outside, shaking with anticipation to see what mom concocted. We couldn't wait to see her.

We lived only a mile from our school—Garland Christian Academy— so Mom would pack away all her little Tupperware containers into a big cardboard box, put our little brother and sister (Johnny and Abby) in their double stroller, and walk our lunch to school. Whichever kid sat in the front held the box.

This was no small shoebox either. It was big enough to fit about four shoeboxes. And we were NEVER allowed to throw it away. That was mom's box, and if even the thought of throwing it in the dumpster crossed our minds she might have gone on lunch-making strike. She loved her box.

Like clockwork, at 11:30 A.M. Mom and the kids would round the corner of our parking lot and stroll through the rows of cars with an aroma of goodness in tow. And, like clockwork, the two of us along with a handful of friends would run out to greet them.

## KIDDOS IN TOW

Johnny and Abby were a big hit with our friends. Thanks to a parenting seminar our parents attended, mom ended up pregnant, twice, when we were in Junior High. That was a surprise. When we first found out she was pregnant with Abby, our older sister, Tracy, was so surprised she bawled her eyes out. We think she felt bad for mom. But then Abby came along and she quickly became Tracy's little "blue bonnet." (That's the Texas state flower, just in case you live in one of the forty-nine lesser states and didn't learn that in middle-school history class.)

Then along came Johnny two years later, as we entered the ninth grade. Those days with two additional siblings in the house were crazy—seven people crammed into a 1,100-square-foot house with only three bedrooms and one full bathroom. Abby and Johnny took turns at night sleeping in bed with us. They had nowhere else to go. But we loved it—snuggling up with those two munchkins at night was one of our favorite things.

When it came to Mom making lunches, it was a family affair. Johnny and Abby loved to help. They couldn't wait for mom to put them in the stroller and head our way.

When Mom took the turn from the sidewalk on Lavon Drive to the parking lot of our high school, all we could see was her pushing the stroller with that big box on top of two little legs with two tiny hands wrapped around it.

"Aww, that is so cute," the girls would say. They loved to see the kids too, especially Johnny. He was a little motor mouth, and you couldn't quite make out what he said. Fortunately, he had his older sister Abby as a full-time interpreter.

"I jumpon a jumpleen," he'd say.

"Do what?" they'd reply.

"He wants you to know he likes jumping on his trampoline," Abby would respond.

## FEEDING HER BOYS

Our buddies knew to stay away from our lunch. If any of them even thought about touching that box, it was not going to end well for them. I (Jason) think Josh Stanberry got an ear full of Cheetos one day—but I don't really remember.

Do you ever have random thoughts such as, "I wonder what that stranger at the table next to me would think if I chewed up this crab cake and blew it into his ear," or "Do you think that guy would be mad if I stirred his shrimp-n-grits with my finger?" Well, the high school lunchroom is where you execute thoughts like that. And we had a few buddies who were on the receiving end.

Mom would hand off the box while our friends hugged her and the kids. She'd have this big smile on her face like she just ran a race and came out victorious. She never really said much, but we could tell from the look on her face she loved doing it. This, to her, was living—and it was a way she brought a little bit of heaven into our lives.

Looking back we can see this simple act of faithfulness fueled our mom—to know her boys were taken care of and she was appreciated for it. That's it—so simple, but so powerful. She wasn't trying to save the world; she was just faithful right where God placed her and to the people He put in her life.

## UNSUNG HERO

It reminds us of the unsung hero in all four Gospels where Jesus fed the 5,000. After He'd been preaching all day, His disciples told Him to send the people away so they could get food, which was probably more *their* desire than it was the crowds'—because the people were hanging on His every word.

We can just hear the disciples now, "Dude, I'm starving! When do you think He's going to be done? Who wants to tell Him to wrap this thing up?" (Jason: If David were around he would've been leading that charge.)

But Jesus, always one step ahead of his guys, responded, "Why don't *you* give them something to eat."

Boom. The disciples saw the need, and Jesus saw the opportunity—for heaven to touch earth through *them*. The hunger of the crowd became a moment for Jesus to practically manifest through His disciples, "Thy kingdom come, Thy will be done, on earth as it is in heaven."

But how? How could these guys provide enough food for that many people? It would take six month's income to buy enough bread just for everyone to have a bite. It was an impossible situation—there was no way they could execute what Christ told them to do. Not even a chance.

Of course, we have the luxury to see how it all worked out, but they didn't. They had no clue what was coming. The more they focused on the problem, the bigger the problem got. But the minute they looked to the Person, Jesus, the solution to their problem presented itself.

"What do you have?" Jesus asked.

The account in the Gospel of John tells us that after searching the crowd, Andrew found a little boy who had five small loaves and two fish—enough for a few tuna fish sandwiches.

Jesus took the loaves and fish, prayed over them in front of the crowd, and after breaking the loaves, He told the disciples to distribute them to the crowd. And the more food they gave away the more food they had—it was incredible. Twelve full baskets later, the crowd was fed, and the disciples had leftovers.

Heaven touched earth in that moment as these hungry people had an encounter with the power of God, all because a little boy was willing to give Jesus what little he had. He'd showed up with enough food for himself and possibly a friend. But after Jesus got ahold of what he had, it was enough to feed thousands.

## WHO PACKED YOUR LUNCH?

The story is good enough if we just leave it at that. But we believe the unsung hero of this miracle was not the disciples or even this little boy—it was the boy's mother. There were probably a lot of kids in the crowd that day, but one kid's mom packed a lunch.

We can imagine earlier that day the little guy running into the house to tell his mom Jesus was coming through town. "Can I go see him, mom? Please let me go!"

"Sure, that will be fine," she responds. "But you're not going anywhere until I pack you a lunch."

This mother, whom we never got to see and whose name we never even know, packed a lunch that became the seed for an incredible miracle. She became the unseen hero of one of the greatest miracles in recorded history. She had no idea the lunch she packed for her boy would be unpacked by the Savior of the world.

## RIVERS

Oswald Chambers once said, "A river touches places that its source knows nothing of." This mom was the source for her boy, and he was able to touch the lives of more than 5,000 people when he gave what he had to Jesus.

To us, this mom was a bridge—an unsung hero who brought divine connection so the work could get done. She packed a lunch privately so

Christ could unpack it publicly. Heaven connected to earth that day, and peoples' lives were radically changed because Momma was faithful to simply pack a lunch.

So often in today's culture, simple acts of faithfulness like this are minimized and not recognized, but Jesus can use them to do incredible miracles. Our Mom touched our lives, and we're still talking about her faithfulness today. She's not with us anymore, but we'll never forget her faithfulness, even when nobody else was watching. We know she was greeted in heaven with a host of witnesses who hugged on her much like we used to in that old high school parking lot. We can see the smile on her face right now as she tells them, "Wait 'till you meet my boys!"

When we encourage believers to stand in the gap we do it with an eye to our mom—the faithful saint who made an indelible impact on our lives. What God has done with us publicly is simply a testimony of what she did for us privately, faithfully, every day we were in high school and for our whole lives.

But Mom didn't have to stand in the gap alone—she had some help along the way …

CHAPTER 10

# TEENAGER MOMENTS

Growing up as preacher's kids, we lived in a whole-church experience 24/7, so church became a little too familiar to us. Why would we crave a vibrant relationship with God when our dad got paid to have one, right? Probably the most fervent praying we did was over one of Mom's epic lunches at school.

To us, church didn't seem all that cool. In fact, it seemed pretty much the opposite of cool. Our small church met in several different places, which required us to set up the night before. While our friends went to the movies or the mall on Saturday nights, we were often setting up chairs in a school gym, creating an improvised altar out of a balance beam and white sheets. Afterward, we'd drive home and watch reruns of Mr. Belvedere while pouting about what dorks we were.

We both gave our lives to Jesus at the age of twelve years. But God didn't become truly the center of our lives until several years later when He brought a couple men to us at just the right time to wake us up, set us on our feet, and get us moving in the right direction.

When we were sixteen years old, our dad lost the church because of his involvement in the pro-life movement. It forced our family to visit other churches, which was as foreign to us as eating blowfish or caviar.

## STEP UP

The first church we visited was Sachse First Baptist, a small country church about forty minutes from Dallas. It was at this church God dropped a "hitch pin" in place specifically designed for the two of us. As we left the service that first day, a tall athletic-looking guy walked up to us and said, "Hey, my name is Todd Foster. You guys should come back to church tonight and hang out with me."

Todd was the youth pastor and had a confident air about him that drew us right in. He was in his early twenties and just out of college where he played basketball. Our sister Tracy thought he was the cutest thing she ever saw outside of Kirk Cameron. All we cared about was learning his bicep workout—those suckers were massive.

We came back to Sachse First Baptist that night and heard Todd speak with a fire for God we had never heard from someone so young. He didn't look like the typical preacher with a fat necktie and pants hiked up to his armpits to keep his muffin top from spilling over. He was cool, at least cool enough for a few young teenagers to think he was *the man*.

We were impressed. We went to church the following Sunday night and heard Todd preach again. There was something in him that resonated deep inside us—we saw in him the kind of Christian we wanted to become. He was an awesome basketball player and used his talent to bring a lot of young men around him to Jesus. Because we were athletes ourselves, this made a divine connection for us.

We were already following Jesus, but we were not on fire for the Lord like he was. Seeing that fire burning in him began to kindle a fire in us. And the more we were around him, the more the fire was stoked.

We soon found ourselves wanting to hang out with him all the time.

We didn't realize it then, but God placed Todd in our lives to fan the embers of faith in our hearts, those smoldering coals needed to be set ablaze. And He knew just what it took to attract a couple teenage jocks to a guy who would stoke that fire.

Todd's leadership challenged us in ways unlike anyone. For starters, he could beat us in one-on-one basketball. Our dad would try to play us, but he was more like a floor mat we walked on with ease (Ha!). But Todd had this pure lefty jumper with a nice first step that made our defense useless. But even more, he challenged us in our faith to step up and be strong men of God.

We'll never forget how he pulled us aside one time and said, "Boys, when are ya'll gonna just step up and be the leaders God has called you to be?"

Wow. Our dad asked that of us before, but it shook us to the core when it came from Todd. When he spoke to us it, was like God gave him the keys to unlock a special place in our hearts where heaven could invade earth. Todd talked to us as if the Lord gave him direct access into our minds. How in the world did he seem to always know just what to say to bring conviction and inspiration at the same time?

Looking back, we realize God used Todd to stand in the gap for us, the gap of an apathetic Christian life. But we didn't have to travel that road for long because Todd loved us enough to stand up and step in. Thanks to him, we were able to have clear direction in our lives before we went off to college.

## A LITTLE RUST WON'T HURT

Another person God used early in our lives was a man by the name of Rusty Thomas. We'll never forget the first Sunday we met him. It was around the year 1985, and Rusty and his wife Liz came to minister to our little church. But he wasn't there to simply preach as much as he was there to do a dramatic presentation of Jesus—like straight up Broadway drama style. We'd never seen anything like it before.

He jumped on stage and began acting out some of the stories of Jesus, yelling with passion as he echoed the words of Christ. He cried, laughed hysterically (like the Joker from Batman laugh), fought the air, and stared in silence (dead silence—awkward pause silence—like *when's he gonna say something* silence). He could create any emotion he wanted on stage—it was fun to watch.

Then he'd open his Bible and bring the application. We knew Dad loved it, because if Rusty could keep his twin boys sitting motionless for forty minutes, he was doing something right—or supernatural. That Sunday became the first of many.

Over the years, after Dad lost the church and became the National Director of Operation Rescue, one of his first moves was to bring Rusty on board as his right-hand man. Rusty was a powerhouse of a street preacher—and still is. Seeing him preach the Word of God so passionately gave us a glimpse of what "zeal for the Lord" looked like. Dad wanted him next to him as often as possible.

## ZEAL IN ACTION

Rusty became one of our dad's closest friends. But even more, he became one of ours. That's hard to say for a guy nearly twenty-five years older than we are. Rusty would come to town and stay at our house when we were teenagers, and he would stay up until the wee hours of the morning talking with us about things we didn't want to say to Dad (or didn't have the guts to). And there wasn't a conversation we had where he wasn't armed with his Bible.

We'd say something, and Rusty would open his Bible real fast, flip through a few pages, put his finger on a passage and just start laughing. Then in his passionate voice, he'd say, "Oh Lord! There it is!! This is exactly what you want to say to these boys, Father!!!" (We can't put enough exclamation points to emphasize his passion.)

He'd look us both in the eyes and then read God's word to us. He'd pause for emphasis, make eye contact, and wait for us to nod yes. He didn't want us to just hear the words—he wanted us to internalize what God was saying. He stared at us with eyes like Aslan until he knew we had taken it all in. Then he'd close his Bible and dig in. Sometimes it was a rebuke we needed. Other times it was a gentle reminder to stay on the right path. But most of the times, it was a dauntless encouragement to become warriors for the Lord.

Those were some of the most impactful conversations of our lives. To this day, we still remember them, and when he comes to town even now, we can't wait to spend time with Rusty. After our mom passed away, we organized a dinner for all the people who flew in for her funeral. When Rusty arrived, we were like little magnets, we couldn't stay away from him. He could hardly enjoy his food because of all the questions we asked. In the middle of our conversation, we thought about mom. She would have loved to see Rusty pouring into us just like he did back in our little house in Dallas as she whipped up her famous eggs and cheese grits during our late-night talks.

For us, Rusty became the man God used to do His work in our hearts. It was as if he had every piece of spiritual farm equipment and knew exactly which one to use at the exact time we needed it. And we're so thankful he did.

## UPSTREAM DOWNSTREAM

Rusty and Todd played pivotal roles in our lives to get us where we are today. God brought them at just the right time to stand in the gap for us, bringing the vital connection He wanted to have with us.

Maybe you've had a Todd or Rusty in your life too. Right now would be a good time to reach out and tell them how much you appreciate them. But also think about stepping into the life of a young person around you.

All of us need an upstream and a downstream—people who are pouring into us and people into whom we are pouring. In this way, we become a bridge for people, as others have been a bridge for us.

Our times with Rusty and Todd also remind us that whenever two or more are gathered, Christ is there. These men truly invited Christ into our teenaged presence.

Sometimes adults tend to assume young people don't notice them— or aren't interesting to them—but our full presence with them invites the presence of Christ into their lives and marks them forever. It's a worthy work God wants to do through us in the fertile fields of youth.

# CHAPTER 11

# SCHOOLHOUSE ROCK

We used to homeschool all our kids. That is, until we realized some of them were just like us—way too extroverted. And we realized, had our parents tried to homeschool us when we were in high school, we might have left for an adventure like the "Goonies," running away in search of Chester Copperpot's hidden treasure.

Regardless, it was tough watching some of our kids go to school for the first time. The one thing that gave us hope was remembering how God brought faithful people into our lives when we were at school—people who said just the right thing at just the right time. They all encouraged us to center our lives on the Lord.

And often the simple things can have the biggest impact on people.

It didn't take long for me (David) to see this happen with my youngest son, Chase. He came home on his last day of the first grade at his new school with his thumb in his mouth (still working on that!) and a note clenched in his little fist.

Dear Chase,

I am so glad you joined our class this year. You are an impressive young man. Keep up your wonderful work ethic and desire to succeed. Most of all, keep up your Bible reading and love for God.

I hope you will look back on your first-grade experience and remember sweet moments of laughter and love.

I look forward to seeing you next year. Be sure to come visit me.

Love you,

Mrs. Russell

I could tell her kind words impacted his tender, eight-year-old heart. But not only him, she impacted us. Knowing she took the time to invest in the spiritual life of our son was humbling.

It reminded me of a time when I was in high school and one of the teaching pastors said something that impacted me in much the same way.

I had just arrived at the gym to watch the girls' basketball game before dressing out to play our game afterward. I plopped down on the front row, sporting my best shirt, a tie, and neatly pressed khaki pants (thanks, Mom). Pastor Denny Smith came and sat right next to me.

"David, you're a trophy," he said. "And you're going to be placed on one of two mantles—the Lord's or the devil's. The choice is yours. Which one will it be?"

He slapped me on the knee, gave me a really big smile, got up, and walked away.

Uh—what?

I had just rolled into the gym with my brother after blasting MC Hammer on the fifteen-inch woofers in our 1967 Volkswagen Bug on the way to the gym. All I was thinking about was my basketball game. Pastor Denny was thinking about my life.

The girls' game disappeared in my mind as I pondered that thought, "Whose mantle am I on?" I didn't notice Sarah Boyd's layup, Becky Harn's jump shot, or Stephanie Thompson's rebounds anymore—all I thought about was which mantle I wanted to be on. (Jason: All I thought about is why Sarah's sister, Amanda, missed that wide-open jumper!)

"The choice is yours," he'd said. His reassuring smile communicated to me, "I believe in you David. I know you'll make the right choice. I'm confident in you."

I can't tell you who we played that night or if we won or how many points I scored, but I'll never forget those words. Heaven touched earth for me—with one simple knee slap and a smile. That night continues to remind me to be God's trophy, on His mantle, for His glory.

In the same way, Pastor Denny connected heaven to earth in my life, Mrs. Russell did for my son Chase. He may not realize it now, but one day he'll look back and remember the investment she made.

> *Like apples of gold in settings of silver is a word spoken in right circumstances. (Proverbs 25:11)*

## WORDS THAT ENCOURAGE

Faith comes by *hearing*. The words we say can either ignite faith in others or extinguish it. That is how powerful our words are. They either kill or heal. The choice is ours.

In my (Jason's) family, we have this little tradition where every month or so we'll go around the dinner table and take turns saying nice things about each other. It's our attempt to help our kids get along (you don't sense any desperation, do you?). One by one they take turns saying one nice thing about their brothers and sisters. The goal is to teach them not only to say nice things but to learn to listen as well.

Our second son Jake loves it when we do this. He's our most sensitive kid—probably destined to be a pastor or marriage counselor one day. I joke with him every now and then and tell him I'm raising my future pastor.

Jake lives for and loves relationships—with everyone. And if something is even remotely out of whack relationally, he can't sit still until it's made right. If Tori and I have a disagreement, we can rest assured we'll hear Jake in the background, "Mom, Dad—you guys need to smooch!"

As is true with most young families, drives in the car can sometimes be more like "rumbles in the jungle." In the middle of an epic car battle one day with bickering going back and forth, Jake, who was probably eight-years-old at the time, waited until a small moment of silence and said, "Dad, can we say nice things?"

Even at his young age, little Jakey understood the power of kind words.

## TEAM WORK

This little tradition actually dates back to our senior year of baseball at Garland Christian Academy. Our coach would get all us players in a circle at the end of every practice, and one by one, we took turns pointing out something good we saw in a teammate. Guys with sweat rings on their hats, dirt stains on their shirts, and stinky bodies that screamed "please wash me now" all took turns complimenting their fellow team-mates. It was one of the most powerful team-building and bonding experiences we ever had.

The impact that made on us individually and as a team was immea-surable. To have another player your same age look you in the eye and say what he appreciated about your effort that day was remarkable. Needless to say, we had few disputes on our team that year.

I remember one gathering being much different from the others. David and I showed up late because we attended the funeral of our close friend who took his life a few days before. We were able to practice only for about an hour or so, doing all the skills and drills we normally did. When we circled up after the workout, Coach Greg said, "Okay, boys. Let's go around the circle and point something out that we appreciated about a teammate today."

There was a long pause, which was typical for high school athletes. Doing something like this was never easy.

Our sophomore second baseman, Aaron Leach, broke the silence. "To see what David and Jason have been through," he said, "and yet how they still showed up to practice and worked as hard as they've worked—it's an example to me. I hope to be a leader just like them when I'm an upperclassman."

Our assistant coach, Larry Horner, chimed in. "You guys have been good leaders on this team," he said as his voice quivered, trying to hold back tears. "You make my job as a coach such a joy. I love you guys."

Several other players followed suit, and the next thing we knew, we were showered with words of encouragement from our teammates. Then they gathered around us and prayed. By the time it was over, we were all choked up.

This little practice was so impactful in my life I incorporated it into my own family.

## THE POWER OF LISTENING WELL

My turn! My turn!

This is David. I can't have a chapter in our book about schoolteachers and the power of our words without mentioning my wife, Lori. She's a great teacher—she homeschooled our kids. And she constantly encourages people with her words. But, I've discovered it's not always what she says but rather how she listens that bridges heaven and earth for many people.

Anyone who's met her will tell you she's possibly the nicest person they've ever met. There's nothing like being married to a person who convicts you all the time just by the way she lives.

When I first met her, I thought, "there's just no way she's that kind and genuinely interested in everything I have to say." I'm sure I was saying all kinds of stupid stuff back then (Jason: Yea, you were). But the way she sat there and listened to me, hanging on my words and listening from the heart was so attractive to me. When it was her turn to talk, she just said one kind thing after another. I had never met anyone like her. Was she real?

I married her as quickly as I could. I couldn't let her get nabbed by some other dude. Since then I have had the privilege of witnessing how Lori's gift of listening well truly brings heaven to earth.

## LISTENING TO SHOW GOD'S LOVE

Take one Christmas, for example. We were at my sister's house in Dallas in the middle of a sugar binge the likes you've never seen before (Jason and I have a strong affinity for sugar cookies with white icing). The tree was filled with glittery balls, homemade schoolhouse decorations, and enough tinsel to start a forest fire. Bing Crosby was on the radio, and cinnamon rolls were in the oven (the good kind, with layers of cream cheese icing!). I can't remember what Lori was doing at the time (probably drinking Earl Gray by the fire); all I remember is sitting on the couch talking with an old family friend, Pat Quinn.

Good ole' Pat. He was one of the first people who came to our church back in 1982. He instantly became our most faithful member and became a part of our family. He didn't miss a single, family event—every birthday party, holiday meal, and even our weekly Sunday night meal featuring mom's famous cheese grits. Boy, those were good!

Pat was a faithful man. He worked at a department store for more than thirty years and lived in the same studio apartment for just as long. He never married and didn't have any family in Dallas, so every holiday he spent with us.

On this particular Christmas, while sitting on the couch with me at my sister's house, Pat tipped back his New York Yankees hat, scratched the top of his gray head, leaned my direction and whispered, "You know, David, your wife is the only person I've ever met who makes me feel like I'm the only person in the world when I talk to her."

Wow! His words were both encouraging and convicting at the same time. Encouraging because the girl he was talking about was my bride. Convicting because I'd known him more than thirty years and he never once said that about me.

Since that Christmas, Lori has made hundreds (probably thousands) of people feel the same way. And God has touched each of them, in small ways and big. Of course, she'd never say this about herself—she's just being who it is God made her to be. But her life serves as an example of the power of a listening ear and a kind word to give a little touch of heaven to people here on earth.

All of us have the ability to invest in those around us, to say kind things, and listen well. If Todd and Rusty can do it, if Mrs. Russell and Pastor Denny can do it, if little Jakey and Lori can do it—then we can all do it.

# CHAPTER 12

# MISS NORMA

Many people know our dad as a nationally recognized, outspoken pro-life leader—a fearless warrior in what some people call the "culture wars." But that's not how he sees himself, and it's certainly not how we see him. To us he's a loving father, a faithful husband, and a bold witness for God; yet he's still human, like any of us. A man with feet of clay. Not only that, but the minute he sits down anywhere—and we mean anywhere—he's probably going to fall asleep. There's nothing like watching our dad passed out, snoring on someone's couch after being invited over for dinner. We shared many embarrassing moments as he woke up, wiped the drool from his cheek, and wondered where on earth he was.

One day, Dad sat on the couch at my (David's) house and told us a story that kept us all awake. He told us about the moment God used his brokenness to pierce the heart of Norma McCorvey, Jane Roe of the infamous *Roe v. Wade* Supreme Court Decision legalizing abortion. Of course, we'd heard many times before about how he and Norma—or Miss Norma as we called her—struck up a friendship and later shared a full-page story in *Time* magazine about her conversion to Christianity. But what we didn't know was how God used his own public rebuke to soften her hardened heart the most.

By her own admission, Miss Norma was an alcoholic, drug user, a liar, and a cheater. But that's why Dad understood her so well—he was the same for much of his life. Yet Jesus stepped in and changed everything for him, and he wanted that for Norma, too. But during the early 1990s, when Dad first met her, she was struggling through life, trying to make an income and battling chemical addictions.

She eventually went public with her identity as Jane Roe, hoping to gain some notoriety and make some cash. At the time, she also had a lesbian partner, even though she was pregnant three times through relationships with men. She desperately needed Jesus, but all she thought she needed was money. She eventually jumped at the opportunity when Harper Collins offered her a publishing contract to write a book about herself, titled, *I Am Roe.*

After the book was released, Dad heard Miss Norma was scheduled to appear at a local establishment called Café Society for a book signing. This was back before the Internet was in full effect, so moments like this were a big deal. Tons of media were in attendance, and a pretty large crowd gathered to hear what she had to say. Dad was across the street waiting for Norma to speak. Then, during a long pause in her speech, he shouted, "Norma McCorvey, you should be ashamed of yourself. You are responsible for the deaths of thirty-five million babies. How dare you desecrate their blood by selling a book!"

Wow. Can you imagine being Norma at that moment?!

His words pierced deep into her heart. Dad could see she was visibly shaken.

## WORDS THAT WOUND

"My heart, when I saw that, it crushed me," Dad said. "I felt really bad. It's not that it was wrong, and it was not that it didn't need to be said. I saw such an effect on her. That's what hurt me: that I hurt her in some way. I don't know how to explain it any better than that, or how to wrap words around it. I knew that I hurt her."

A few months later, Dad set up his ministry office next door to A Women's Choice abortion clinic. And guess who happened to work there? Norma McCorvey. Dad and Norma were neighbors. Their build-ings shared a parking lot, so they saw each other from time to time. Miss Norma frequently took smoke breaks, something with which Dad was very familiar from his past. So, he decided to try talking to her while she puffed away out on the bench by the parking lot. They talked about many things, including his alcoholic past, his love for the Beach Boys, and of course his family.

Norma must have been astonished to discover this fiery preacher the abortion clinic folks nicknamed "Flip Venom" was just a regular guy, easy-going, and not-so-perfect, like herself. This was the side of Dad very few people saw, but she saw it often on her daily smoke breaks. We're still not sure why she was gracious enough to talk to him given how he'd called her out publicly a few months before.

Yet over time, Dad told us he built trust in her. Then one day, the Lord prompted him to talk with her about that day at her book signing. She was sitting on the bench outside during one of her smoke breaks, and he walked up and sat down next to her and said, "Do you remember that time on McKinney Street when I came over during your book sign-ing?" Dad asked.

"Uh, yea," Norma replied.

"Listen, something really crushed me," Dad continued. "And I just want you to know that I saw those words sort of fall into you. I want you to know I'm sorry that those words hurt you."

At that point of telling the story, Dad's eyes clouded with tears as he recalled that conversation. He said Norma began to cry. She told us later she couldn't believe the big bully pro-life activist apologized to her. It was a breakthrough moment for her.

From that day on, their relationship transformed. Norma opened up more and more with each passing day. Dad shared with her about Jesus and how much God loves her, no matter what she did in the past. Norma couldn't believe anyone would love her with her sordid past. She never felt love from her mother or her father, so how could God—who knew each and every one of her sins—love her? But Dad's compassion softened her. And his openness about his own past moved her toward the same God Who forgave him.

Months later, she started attending church. One Saturday night, she attended the church of Pastor Morris Sheats. He delivered a direct, very clear Gospel message. His text was John 3:16. In Norma's heart, it read, "For God so loved Norma, that he sent his one and only son, that whoever believes in him would not perish but have everlasting life."

She struggled in the pew for a while with the Holy Spirit. Then she started to sweat as she felt every eye was on her. Something was breaking apart inside her that made her want to run out of the building.

When Pastor Sheats asked people to come forward to accept Christ, Norma walked to the front, not entirely sure what she was doing. Then, she tells of how she looked into the pastor's eyes, feeling the unconditional love of Jesus for her, and how she was overcome by a sensation, like a wind blowing through her. She started to cry. Then she began to weep. She confessed her sins and accepted Christ as her Savior right then and there.

When she told Dad the news, he encouraged her to be baptized as a public proclamation of the faith that had taken hold of her that day. And to his surprise, she asked him to do the honors.

Because Dad didn't have his own church at the time, we didn't have a place to baptize her. Dad asked some friends if he could use their pool. We watched as Dad stepped into that backyard swimming pool surrounded by reporters and camera crews ready to publicize this historic event.

Wearing my (David's) red tie and Jason's denim blue shirt (we wouldn't allow him to be on primetime television wearing anything from his own closet), Dad read from Isaiah 61—much like Jesus did when he began his teaching ministry in Luke 4. "The Spirit of the Lord is on me, because he has anointed me to preach good news to the poor …" Dad placed a cloth over her face, leaned her backward, and fully immersed her.

Jane Roe washed away.

Norma McCorvey emerged brand new.

## NO MORE SHAME

For the following months, Dad spent a lot of time mentoring Miss Norma in her budding faith. He told us she felt like she could never look God in the face and not be ashamed because of the things she did and the babies killed as a result of her involvement in *Roe v. Wade.*

But he kept reminding her of Psalm 34:5, "Those who look to him shall be radiant; their faces are never covered in shame."

He assured her Jane Roe, the poster child of the pro-choice movement, was dead. Norma McCorvey, the born-again believer in Jesus Christ, was alive. She jumped from that lying poster into the arms of Jesus and was now set apart to be a voice for all of the voiceless babies safe in their mother's womb. That became her new identity as a child of God.

## WIDE AWAKE NOW

Miss Norma went from the path of destruction to the path of restoration—largely because our Dad coupled boldness with brokenness. He said what he felt God wanted him to say at the book signing that day. His bold words helped break up hardened ground. But his heart was broken for her—he wanted her to be restored, just as he was. He wanted her to be connected with the very God who loved her.

The next few years were amazing, as the once harsh, scowling Ms. Norma became a soft, smiling beacon of light in our lives and in the lives of everyone she touched. She even brought over her former lesbian partner, Connie, for dinner at our house. Eventually, Connie surrendered her life to Jesus as well. That time Dad sent us to Wal-Mart for a blow-up swimming pool so he could baptize her, too!

# CHAPTER 13

# A TALE OF THREE PETERS

When we were kids, our dad used to say, "Boys, we are called to walk the narrow road for Christ—and that means there are ditches on both sides." He learned this lesson well with Miss Norma!

For us today, if we are going to be a bridge for the Lord, then we've got to walk the narrow way that leads to life—not just for us but for others as well. One thing we've found through the years is the way for us to stay on the narrow path is to walk in *love*. But the ditches of *anger* and *fear* are always one step away on either side.

We've discovered that boldness apart from brokenness leads to anger. Yet brokenness apart from boldness leads to fear. To faithfully be a bridge today requires both boldness *and* brokenness—to have one without the other lands us in a ditch off the path of the narrow way, rendering us ineffective for God.

If we are bold for God's truth but not broken over our sin we'll operate out of a spirit of anger. This makes us a bully, which leaves others disconnected from God—because the truth we're speaking can't get past the angry look on our faces.

Boldness apart from brokenness makes a **bully**. This is what anger produces.

If we're broken over our sin but not bold for God's truth we'll operate out of a spirit of fear. This makes us a bystander, which also leaves people disconnected from God—because we're too afraid to share the truth that can set them free.

Brokenness apart from boldness makes a **bystander**. This is what fear produces.

But if we're both bold *and* broken we'll operate out of a spirit of love. This is what gives us the power to faithfully stand in the gap and bring divine connection to disconnected people.

Boldness *and* brokenness make us a **bridge** connecting heaven to earth for those around us. This is what love produces.

## PETER ~~IN THE DITCH~~ ON THE NARROW ROAD

We see this balance played out in the life of Peter, a man who fell into the ditch on both sides but finally found his way back onto the narrow way and was used powerfully by God.

Poor Peter gets such a bad rap at times. Seriously, he was probably the oldest disciple and by far the boldest among them. He was the only guy willing to jump out of the boat and walk on water with Jesus, he was ready to fight the minute his friends were in trouble, and he wasn't scared to speak up when his buddies were silent. Peter's life reminds me (Jason) a lot of my eight-year-old daughter. She's not scared to say anything to anyone at any time—especially when company comes over. Maybe you have a kid like that.

But, as is often the case, our greatest strength can be our greatest weakness. Fortunately for us, the Bible doesn't pull any punches when describing Peter's weaknesses and mess-ups.

Peter was a naturally bold guy. But we see repeatedly in the Gospels how he lacked the genuine humility only a person broken over his or her sin can have—the vital attribute a bold warrior such as Peter desperately needed.

We pick up his story the night Jesus and His disciples had their last meal together, just after the Lord told them He would be betrayed, and they would all fall away. Peter—in his typical bold fashion—declared, "Even if all fall away on account of you, I never will."

Of course, Peter wouldn't fall away, right? He was the top dog in Christ's inner circle. Of the twelve disciples, he was one of just three who got to see Jesus transfigured on the mountain. He was the one who first recognized Jesus as the Messiah. And he was the guy Christ named as a rock to help build the church. You can tell a lot about people by how they handle a compliment. This one appeared to get to Peter's head because it might have stoked the fire of his inner self-sufficiency.

But Jesus knew what He was doing and where He was going with Peter. He knew Peter's weakness better than Peter did. So, Jesus responded to his bold claim, saying, "Truly I tell you, this very night, before the rooster crows, you will deny me three times."

Peter wasn't buying it. "Even if I have to die with you, I will never disown you" (Matthew 26:31–35).

When we read this story, we can almost see Jesus at this moment, sighing with the thought, *Peter, you have no idea what's coming.*

After they finished dinner, Jesus took His disciples with Him to the Garden of Gethsemane. His betrayal was just moments away, and He wanted to pray. When they arrived, He told the disciples to sit down while He went to another place to pray alone. He then asked His top three guys to come along with Him. Peter was among them again.

Can you imagine how Peter felt? Looking at the last three years with Jesus and considering some of the conversations they had, maybe he thought to himself, *Jesus always wants me close to Him. I can't wait to see how amazing it's going to be when He takes the throne of Israel. I wonder what it feels like to be second in command of an entire kingdom. I'll find out soon enough.*

Of course, those thoughts faded pretty fast as he fell fast asleep and started drooling on a rock. As a matter of fact, all three of Jesus's closest buds zonked out hardcore. They couldn't even honor the one thing Christ told them to do—"Keep watch and pray." Nope. Not gonna' happen. Three times this happened.

## ANGER, DITCH NO. 1

Little did Peter know that allowing his flesh to overrule his spirit was a recipe for disaster. His first lesson was about to play itself out. In the middle of his log-sawing episode, it happened—the enemy Christ warned them about showed up in full force, weapons and all.

Startled awake, Peter grabbed his sword and swung with all his might at the head of one of the men, cutting off his ear. *Not on my watch*, Peter probably thought to himself.

Now, we'll give Peter a hall pass for missing—he'd just been awakened. You'd have terrible aim too. He was probably going for a headshot and hit the ear. He either had a crazy head-rush from just waking up and missed the dude's head or the guy ducked. Either way, it was a swing and a miss.

But this is where the story gets interesting. Jesus told Peter to put his sword away. If you "live by the sword you will die by the sword," Jesus told him (Matthew 26:52). In other words, if we want to take people's heads off, we'll never get their hearts. And *that's* what Jesus was after.

Peter was not yet broken, so in his boldness, he reached for the wrong weapon. He was operating in the physical rather than the spiritual. Thankfully, Christ taught him that instead of trying to *hurt* we must seek to *heal* as He touched the man's ear and restored him.

**This was Peter the bully. He was bold but not broken. Operating out of a spirit of anger, he was ready to fight when the mob showed up.**

Peter was definitely willing to stand in the gap, but he did it in the wrong spirit, which disqualified him from being the person God could use to bring the plan of Heaven to earth.

## FEAR, DITCH NO. 2

Yet, Peter still had more to learn because the pendulum of life's lessons often swings from one extreme to the other.

With blood still on his sword, he watched Jesus willingly walk with the mob toward the city. He followed, but this time at a distance. He wanted to see what would happen, but he didn't want to be a part of it. No longer was he ready to go all in as he once was. Truth be told, we'd all be tempted to do the same thing.

The mob led Jesus to the house of Caiaphas, the High Priest, who was probably still holding a grudge against Jesus for disrupting his money-making business in the temple, among other things. Standing against the leaders of the day was simply not something you did back then. It got Jesus into a lot of trouble.

While all this happened, Peter sat in the courtyard, warming himself by the fire. Notice how cowardice and comfort replaced courage and commitment when Peter lost his boldness. He was more concerned about staying comfortable than he was about standing with courage.

As the fire crackled and warmed Peter's hands, a servant girl approached and said, "You also were with Jesus of Galilee."

He answered, "I don't know what you're talking about." Liar liar, pants on fire.

Another one approached and said in front of everyone, "This fellow was with Jesus of Nazareth." Peter denied it again, this time more emphatically—"I don't know the man!"

But they weren't buying it, and finally they said, "Surely you are one of them; your accent gives you away."

That's when Peter put the final nail in the coffin as he began to curse along with his denial.

It's as if Peter said, "You still think I'm one of them, huh? Well, I'll prove it to you, you @#%!! I don't know the man!"

We believe one of the most certain ways to disassociate from Jesus is to use profanity. Most people will assume you don't know Him, just like they did with Peter.

At that very moment, a rooster crowed. Peter denied the very man he swore to protect.

"Then Peter remembered the words Jesus spoke: 'Before the rooster crows, you will disown me three times.' And he went outside and wept bitterly" (Matthew 26:69–75).

Peter knew it was over. He failed, miserably. He had just denied his best friend in the world, the man he claimed to be king.

Jesus was put on public trial, humiliated in front of an entire city, flogged, and ultimately crucified. The Gospel doesn't tell us what Peter was doing during this time. We have no idea where he was after he denied Jesus in the courtyard.

**This was Peter the bystander. He was broken but not bold. Operating out of a spirit of fear, he was ready to run when the angry mob showed up.**

## TIME TO GET UP!

The next time we hear of Peter came from the angel standing at Christ's empty tomb when he mentioned him by name. He knew Peter needed to be restored from his failure, not destroyed by it. So, the angel said to the three women there, "… He has risen! He is not here. See the place where they laid Him. But go, tell His disciples and PETER …" (Mark 16:6–7). God is so gracious to us when we mess up.

Can you imagine how Peter felt when these ladies told him the angel mentioned him by name? He was probably thinking, "Wait, I thought I was done. You mean I'm still on the team?"

After Peter checked out the empty tomb for himself, he went back into Jerusalem where the other disciples were hiding. Then, out of the blue, Jesus appeared! All of them freaked out—they thought He was a ghost. But Jesus calmed them down after He showed them His nail-scarred hands and feet.

We know Peter was in the room that day, but we don't have any information that Jesus spoke to him directly. Can you imagine how this felt for Peter? He might have thought, "Uh, are we okay? I mean—I know what you heard me say in the courtyard …"

Awkward.

Jesus was not done with Peter. He showed up again a few days later, this time in Galilee by a lake—the very lake in which Peter decided earlier to go fishing. It appeared Peter knew he needed to go back to fishing because his days as a disciple were at an end.

Jesus stood on the shore and called out to him in the same way He did when He recruited Peter three years before—"Throw your net to the other side of the boat and you'll find some" (John 21:6). The same result ensued—they caught more fish than they could carry in the net.

Peter realized it was Jesus and jumped out of the boat and swam to shore. Can you sense his urgency? How many of us have hurt someone only to desperately desire to make things right?

Now it was time for Jesus and Peter to talk man to man.

Three times Jesus asked him, "Do you *love* me?" Peter's heart probably felt the sting, reminding him of what he did just days before. All three times, Peter responded the same way, "Yes Lord, you know that I *love* you."

Jesus was teaching Peter the importance of love. No more anger, no more fear—just love for the Savior would enable Peter to be useful to Jesus.

Jesus responded each time to Peter's confession, "Feed My sheep … Take care of My sheep … Feed My sheep."

Now, up to this point, Jesus was the one who was the shepherd feeding the sheep; He referred to Himself like this several times. But now, after Peter's incredible failure, Jesus not only reinstated him but gave him the very mantle He carried—that of a shepherd.

Jesus essentially said to Peter, "You are finally bold *and* broken. So now I commission you to do what I have always done—shepherd people. As I have done so you must also do!" Wow.

Imagine the impact that had on Peter. To fail Jesus like he did but then to be made captain of the team.

## EMPOWERED

In His final words before He was taken back to Heaven, Jesus told Peter and the other disciples to wait in Jerusalem until they were "clothed with power from on high" (Luke 24:49).

Several weeks later, as the disciples were holed up in an upstairs room in Jerusalem, still in danger of being beaten or even killed for believing in Jesus, the moment Jesus told them about happened. It was the Day of Pentecost, when Jews from every nation gathered in Jerusalem, all of them speaking their own dialect. All of a sudden, the sound of a rushing wind filled the room as the Holy Spirit descended upon each of them.

The crowd heard the sound of the wind and gathered where the disciples were. And when they arrived, they were astonished to hear these men speaking in their native languages. Seeing the crowd was utterly confused, wondering how this could be possible, Peter stood to his feet.

Pause here for a moment. Peter could have easily operated out of anger like he did before and scold the crowd without giving them the hope of redemption. They killed Jesus, after all. Or he could have stayed seated out of fear of persecution, or because he was such a failure in the past. But that's not what he did.

Peter stood and addressed them all, speaking in front of thousands of people, knowing full well it could cost him dearly. He did it with a heart full of love for the Savior he failed but who forgave him and set him back on his feet and enlisted him in His kingdom-building effort here on the earth.

That day 3,000 people got radically saved. Bam! Heaven touched earth through Peter. He went from small and insignificant to strong and indispensable for these people because he was willing to stand in the gap and connect these people to the God who created them.

**This was Peter, the bridge. He was both bold and broken. Operating out of a spirit of love, he was ready to stand. When the crowd showed up, he didn't run *after* them or run *from* them, he stood *for* them.**

Peter finally transformed into the man Jesus always knew he could be—a man who was willing to stand in the gap for others so heaven could invade earth through him. God wanted to touch the hearts of those people that day, and He was able to do it because a broken man chose to stand boldly for Him.

# CHAPTER 14

# FAITH THAT FALTERS

Peter's story can teach us a lot about how to walk that narrow way—avoiding the pitfalls of anger and fear. But that knowledge doesn't immunize us from feeling those emotions.

Scripture tells us fear and faith are opposites. They can't peacefully coexist. In any given day, we might experience highs of faith and lows of fear. The beauty is we get to choose which one wins. What will it be? Fear or Faith?

## CALLED OUT

"Are you and your brother anti-gay?"

That was the question I (Jason) was asked on a conference call with our production company.

To put this question in context, we had just agreed in principle to an offer from HGTV for a straight-to-series show with no pilot. But before the long-form contract could be signed, their attorneys had to do the typical background check to make sure they weren't hiring a couple shysters.

During their search, they discovered we were not just real estate entrepreneurs but were also vocal about our faith. That wasn't a problem for them. The issue was we voiced God's values that run against the politically correct mainstream value system, specifically in regard to life and marriage.

Houston, we have a problem.

They discovered an unfavorable article written about us the previous year, villainizing us (specifically David) for speaking publicly about on these two issues. Those were (and still are) hot-button topics of the day, and because we stood for the Biblical definition of both—life begins at conception and marriage is between a man and a woman—the narrative about us in media switched from "two successful Christian entrepreneurs" to "anti-women, gay-bashing extremists."

Wait, there's a verse about that—"Blessed are you when people insult you and persecute you, and falsely say all kinds of evil against you because of Me" (Matthew 5:13). The Bible affirms we are actually blessed when people believe false things about us when standing for God's truth. Good to remember.

## SURPRISE ATTACK

I want to tell you what happened in my heart when I heard that question. You see, up to that point, the two of us were typically bold about our faith and didn't generally have a problem standing for truth. But on this particular occasion, when asked that point-blank question, I felt something I hadn't felt in a long time—FEAR. It was more like stark terror. (It's a good thing David wasn't on the call—he probably would've cried on the other line.)

I felt fear before, but nothing to this magnitude. It was as if a man-pleasing spirit the size of a gorilla jumped on my back. My heart pounded, and my head got hot.

As soon as she asked the question, I heard a little voice in my mind say, "You better be careful how you answer because if you don't give her the right response you're going to lose the platform you and your brother want so bad."

It was true we were planning to use this new reality-show platform God gave us to share Christ with people. We knew whatever fame or notoriety came our way we would redirect it to the Lord. But, that platform was being threatened because the people at HGTV might believe something about us that wasn't true.

I said a quick prayer and then responded, "No, we're not anti-anything. We're pro-Jesus. Which makes us pro-Bible." That response was met with silence on the line, so I continued. For the next five minutes I basically explained that God's blessings are found within His boundaries, and if those boundaries are removed, then His blessings are replaced with burdens. Because we love people, we know how important it is to talk about those boundaries so people can be blessed.

I finished with this, "You don't sell more than 20,000 houses nationwide by discriminating against anyone. That article is a false accusation against us and doesn't paint a true picture of who we are or what we believe. God loves all people and so do we, but He doesn't love all ideas, nor do we."

Her response floored me. "You know, I think there's actually a lot of people at HGTV and the production company who believe like you guys—we just don't talk about it." Of course, they don't. Nobody wants to be falsely accused in today's culture—we get it.

I hung up the phone, wiped my forehead, and thanked God for giving me just the right words to say. "Thank you, Lord, for saving our show," I thought.

## WAITING

Two weeks went by, and we didn't hear from anyone—not the production company, not our agents, not HGTV—nobody. We both thought we were getting dumped. So, we decided to scour the internet and get rid of anything that could be considered "controversial" as best we could. Pretty bold, huh?

HGTV eventually reached back out with a desire to sign us, knowing what was said about us was a twisted narrative. That felt good. All was going well until four weeks into filming and after commercials for our show started to air, when one of the executives called us to let us know an activist group called and was furious we were going to have a show on HGTV.

Here we go again—that same "man-pleasing spirit" jumped on our backs. This time, we decided to draft an email to HGTV explaining our beliefs in an effort to save the show.

Do you want to know what that email said? Essentially, it said, "These are our beliefs, and we won't back off them. However, when we represent HGTV, we'll be quiet about them."

How 'bout them apples? Here we were two "bold" guys acting like blundering idiots because we were scared to lose a platform God was giving us. With that shift, our focus was on the platform we desired instead of the Person (God) who gave it to us in the first place.

We later learned that when you take your focus off the Person of God and put it on the thing He's given you, you become enslaved by that very thing. The one thing we weren't willing to let go was controlling us. It became an idol.

In that brief moment, we turned from God-fearing men into man-pleasing cowards, all because we weren't willing to let go of that thing God placed in our hands.

## THE BEAUTY OF ACCOUNTABILITY

Now, before you burn this book, we have to let you know we decided to send the email to a pastor friend of ours first, before we sent it to HG. We knew not to send it to our dad—we weren't feeling that spiritual! We knew what he would say.

Within three minutes, we got a scathing response. Our friend and pastor rebuked us for our lack of faith and our cowardly effort to try to save our show. He didn't mince words and told us we had no business acting like this and we essentially needed to repent for our man-pleasing spirit.

Oh, snap! Talk about humbling. Needless to say, we never sent that email to HGTV.

The minute we read his response, we were cut to the heart. We knew he was speaking truth, and we needed to repent. We did. Right there on our living room floor, we knelt and asked God to forgive us for taking our focus off Him and putting it on what He gave us.

## BROTHER PETE

At that moment, we felt what Peter must have felt when he became a bystander, promising his best friend in the world, Jesus, he'd never deny Him. But, as we talked about in the last chapter, Jesus knew Peter would deny him before the rooster crowed that day. Sure enough, that very night he denied Jesus three times.

Can you imagine how he must have felt when he heard the rooster crow? We can because, when the ding of that email came through, it was like the rooster was crowing in our ears.

We had no clue that just a short while later we would be fired in front of a watching world and we'd need to stand boldly for the Lord. But God had to first break us of our own self-sufficiency and our man-pleasing spirit. He had to teach us to let go of what we were holding onto and face our fears.

Being broken isn't about sulking in guilt over your sin. And it isn't about God breaking you against your own will like a trainer breaks a horse. It's about recognizing you've sinned against God, repenting, and walking in the humility and power of the Holy Spirit with a heart for others to experience the same restoration. When you're broken like this, you have all the power you need to connect Heaven to earth.

## PREPPED AND READY

In May of that year, several weeks after we almost sent that email, we got a text from the executives at HGTV wanting to get on a call. We knew the pressure from the activist group the previous week was intense, and HG was doing everything they could to hold them at bay. But by that time the pressure was at a fever pitch. We prayed just before we made the call, "Lord, we promised to serve you whatever the cost. We're with you no matter which direction this goes. Please give us strength."

Right out of the gate, the top executive said, "Guys, we're canceling the show." After I (David) picked Jason up from his fetal position and knocked his thumb out of his mouth, I said, "Thank you. Thank you for sticking with us. We know you stuck up for us, and this isn't what you wanted." She replied, "I wasn't expecting to be speechless on this call."

We knew HGTV wanted us on the network—they loved us and wanted to stick with us. We loved them too. But they got bullied by an activist group and caved to the pressure. We've never once faulted them for this.

We told them we loved them and felt bad for the tough decision they had to make. We then explained there was an agenda in culture that demanded silence from Christians, and we had no intention of backing down.

## TIME TO STAND

From that point forward, we went on more talk shows than we can count—FOX, ABC, CNN—all of them. We had no clue what we were going to say; we simply held fast to Luke 21:14, "But make up your mind not to worry beforehand how to defend yourselves. For I will give you words and wisdom that none of your adversaries will be able to resist or contradict."

We learned when you choose to stand boldly for the Lord, the Holy Spirit will give you what to say in that moment, so long as you feel genuine love for those to whom you're speaking. We honestly never felt anger or hatred toward those attacking us. The reason why is because by this time we were broken men. God had already broken us and showed us how pathetic we were on our own, so what right did we have to be hostile to other human beings, no matter how badly they treated us?

I (Jason) remember being on the *Megyn Kelly Show*. We were sitting in a soundproof studio in Charlotte with nothing but a camera and earpieces. The producer came on the line and said, "Welcome to the big leagues, boys. We're live in ten seconds!" I think David may have wet his pants. Not really sure, but I know something was going on.

After she asked David a question, she addressed one right at me. It was surreal because, even while she was talking, I thought to myself, *I have no clue what I'm about to say.* That's a scary place to be. But after I got done with my response, I remember thinking, *Wow, that was actually really good!* HA! Because I knew it wasn't me.

Several weeks later and after more than fifty interviews, the emails and letters started pouring in from Christians all over the world—most of them encouraging us to keep standing in the gap. But several of them humbled us to the core. People who said seeing us stand boldly when so much of the media was against us inspired them to boldly stand in the gap themselves. Of course, we couldn't help but think, "Just wait until you hear how cowardly we really were at one time."

A politician in Texas came up to us after an event where we shared this story and said, "I drafted a piece of legislation that I neglected to put forward for a vote because I was scared of the backlash. But after hearing you guys speak about your 'Peter moment,' I'm inspired to go back and introduce it to get it passed." And he did.

We are a couple of fearful idiots; trust us—so we're not telling you this to float our boat. We share this so you, too, can see what God can do when you choose to stand boldly for Him, even when you're scared to death. Even after you've been too afraid and failed, even when you have no clue what to do or say. When you simply stand in the gap, you become a bridge that brings divine connection so others can experience the power of God. In our case with HGTV, it was simply connecting truth to a disconnected world.

## CHALLENGE MOMENTS

Our HGTV story is simply a larger-scale version of what we still go through on a regular basis in little things all the time. The call to stand in the gap isn't just for the glamorous moments when the cameras are on—it's for daily life when you're standing face to face with the checkout attendant at the grocery store and the dozens of other opportunities that present themselves throughout your day.

While writing this book, I (David) felt a nudge from the Lord to tell a man at the grocery store Jesus loved him. Sure enough, that same old fear rose up in me again, reminding me of that moment years ago when I acted just like Peter in the courtyard, denying Jesus. But I remembered how boldness could be the very thing that connects Heaven to earth in this man's life. So, I said it. He said thank you. And that was it. I walked to my car with a feeling of accomplishment, knowing that at least this time I didn't let my fear keep me from doing what was right. I did my duty. The results were up to God.

What's interesting is that man showed up at my gym to work out a few weeks later, and I didn't even recognize him. He came right up to me and asked if he could talk with me after the workout. I still had no clue this was the guy from the grocery store, but during our talk, he reminded me what I said to him—and it all came back to me.

Miraculously, he opened up with me and said he had been considering suicide and struggled with the value of his life. I immediately prioritized this relationship and began meeting with him for lunch to talk about his identity as a creation of God with immense value and worth. As I write this, we continue to grow in relationship as I do my best to bridge him back to his heavenly Father.

# CHAPTER 15

# FACE YOUR FEAR

This is Tori. I'm married to the better-looking author of this book—Jason. Haha!

I believe with all my heart God uses people to bring His will in heaven down to the earth He created, just like the Lord's prayer says. But, just as the boys talked about in the previous chapter, I have seen firsthand how fear is the one thing that will keep people from helping make the connection. And fear—is the opposite of faith.

Fear has been a fierce enemy of mine for as long as I remember. I grew up the only girl among four boys (dad included) who loved to make me scream. It was even better for them if I peed my pants, which happened on more than one occasion. Rubber spiders, fake snakes, sneaking up on me from behind. It didn't take much. I was such an easy target.

But that was the cute kind of fear. The kind we still die laughing about around the dinner table. The not-so-cute fear that crept in over the years was the real danger. It almost kept me from the good things God had in store.

God put me in a few situations beyond my control to break fear's grip on me.

## JUSTIFYING FEAR

I remember when we first looked at a piece of property in 2004. Jason saw potential. I only saw problems. The property looked so scary. It was surrounded by woods. No street lights. Pitch black at night. No neighbors with kids. And it had a pool of all things—the very thing that makes a pregnant mom with two young kids break out in hives.

In those days Jason traveled often so I stood in front of the house and thought, "We could all die out here and no one would know for days."

I was being a responsible mom, thinking through all the worst-case scenarios. That's what moms are supposed to do, right? But in reality, fear had its grip on me. So, I tried to fight it off with control, like I often did.

Looking back, I feared what I couldn't control, so I tried to control what I feared. It was a vicious cycle.

"No! This is not the one," I told Jason. "It doesn't matter how much you want it. No."

I wanted desperately for him to agree with me and let me have my way. But as the words were leaving my mouth I felt the Holy Spirit say, "You need to give up this control and give it to Me."

That's not the comfort I was looking for, but I knew God was speaking to me.

As I walked around the backyard, I remember praying, "Okay, Lord. I trust you more than I trust myself, so I'm going to give this to You. You know our future, You know our kids, and if You want us to have this house, then allow us to get it. But if we're in danger out here or if somebody is going to drown in this pool, shut every door. I'm not going to try to control anything. I'm just going to give it to You."

That was it. But before I even finished the prayer I felt a weight lift off my shoulders. Although I still wasn't overly excited about getting the house, I felt peace.

## DREAM HOUSE

Well, when I told Jason it was okay to get the house, he went after it like a thoroughbred on race day. A few months later we owned the place.

Lo and behold, the pool that brought me so much anxiety has become one of the best parts of the house. Who would've known how amazing a pool is when your kids are finally waterproof? Hot summer days could be cooled by a quick dip. Play dates with other moms were much easier with a place for kids to get their wiggles out. We've even had a few baptism services in it. And yes, there's no better sound than hearing Jason say at the end of a long day, "pool baths tonight, kiddos!"

A few years later, the lot next to ours went up for sale. My parents bought it and built a house and moved in with my two little brothers. Those dark, scary woods are now filled with people I love. My mom helps me homeschool the kids while dad fixes everything that breaks. And Dad's always willing to run over, even in the middle of the night, if Jason's out of town and I've heard something. (David: I think he still runs over even when Jason *is* home!)

A few years after mom and dad moved in, one of Jason's teammates from college moved his family three doors down. Then David and Lori built a house two doors from him. Jason's roommate from college and his family moved in next door after that, followed by Jason's cousin moving his family to the house next to David. To top it off, my older brother and his family bought a house in the neighborhood, and then my grandpa moved into the house across the street from us. I'm not making this up!

The once-barren streets twelve years ago are now bustling with kids—forty in all if you include a few other young families in the neighborhood. Now, each of our kids gets to do life everyday with their best friends. They have no idea how good they have it.

I didn't see any of this when I stood frozen in fear on that dark scary lot. But God did.

As I reflect on what my family would have missed had I let my fear win the battle, I hear God say, "See what happens when you face your fear and trust Me?!"

I've discovered that our greatest blessings are found only on the other side of our greatest fears. When I faced my fear and chose to trust God, releasing full control to Him, He took over the fight. And now my entire family gets to enjoy the blessing.

## SOMETHING NEW

But you all know how fear works—it's never fully defeated until we're home in heaven. So, while we're here on earth, it's a daily battle for all of us, especially me. This truth came flooding back one fall when a church reached out to Jason and me to speak at their annual marriage retreat.

Me? Speak?

Every time the topic came up, my stomach turned and I felt weak. The very thought made me lose my appetite. I lost ten pounds before the event, which felt like a reward for all the stress. I don't recommend that as a diet plan though. Because the event was a year out, that gave me one full year to live with a gut ache.

Here's the interesting part—at the beginning of the year I always ask the Lord to give me a word. That year He gave me the word "new." With this event coming up, I felt God pushing me to be made new in Him by facing my fears, once again. I wrote in my journal a quote I'd stumbled across:

*Do something every day that scares you.*

God knew the scariest thing in the world for me would be to get up and speak in front of a crowd. So, this is exactly what He cooked up to help me get over my fear. I felt like saying, "Thanks a lot, God."

It didn't help when Jason told me about a research study showing the top five greatest fears—death was number two on the list. You can guess what number one was—public speaking. Wonderful. People would rather die than speak. That's exactly what I needed to hear.

To help break through my fear, I decided to do something that scared me. I've always had a fear of heights, so I took my youngest son, Jake, to the local trampoline park where they have a climbing wall. I climbed as high as I could go, feeling anxious the entire way. Then I jumped. I screamed the entire way down.

Turns out, the thought of jumping was worse than jumping.

And just as the anticipation of jumping is often worse than jumping, I think the anticipation of speaking might be worse than speaking. Jason wanted to discuss it before the event. We'd be talking about something else and he'd say, "You know we ought to consider what we're going to talk about at the marriage conference." But I was clueless. All I could think of was the line from *Finding Nemo*, "Find a happy place, find a happy place, find a happy place."

I reminded myself of times in the past when God conquered my fear, when my faith intersected with God's faithfulness. I thought of our house years before. Yet, I still felt scared. Really scared. God was teaching me to fight through it when I really wanted to run from it.

Two weeks before the marriage conference, we invited a few young couples from our church over so we could do a practice run in our living room. These are people who love me and would never look down on me even if I was the worst speaker who ever lived.

From my vantage point, it went badly. I was so nervous and felt like a bumbling mess. But even though I was scared and doubting myself the entire time, I powered through. One step at a time.

One of the wives came up to me afterward. She was so sweet. "I really got a lot out of what you said," she told me. It felt good, but deep down I was thinking she was probably just being kind.

I wanted so badly to just pull out of the conference and save myself— and those in attendance—from the embarrassment. I even thought about asking God to give me the flu. That would save me. "Let Jason carry this," I thought. "He's the gifted speaker here."

When my emotions calmed down, I confessed, "Lord, I'm sorry. I'm making this all about me, but I know it's all about You."

## JESUS, "TAKE THE WHEEL!"

I never got the flu, so when the date arrived, we boarded a plane out to a rural part of Indiana. The church rented a facility in a small Amish town chock full of horses and buggies lining the streets and parking lots.

As we walked into the hotel, knowing I was about to speak to a room full of people, I jokingly sang the lyrics to "Jesus, Take the Wheel." We both laughed pretty hard, but behind the laugh, I was terrified.

When the time came to speak, I sat up on stage next to Jason as he opened the talk.

Then it was my turn.

As I began to speak, something in my spirit shifted. I felt the power of the Holy Spirit, like I was powered by electricity and was suddenly plugged into an outlet. I wasn't scared anymore. Fear lost its grip on me at that moment.

When I was up there speaking, I felt a breakthrough taking place in real time as I walked toward my fear and not from it.

As I spoke, I realized I wasn't stuttering, I wasn't sweating, and I wasn't paralyzed in fear. I knew I was exactly where I was supposed to be.

After the conference, several women thanked me for what I shared, touched by the message and stories. Because I was open about my nervousness, my obedience to get up there made an impact on people. I'm not looking for more speaking engagements, but now I'm not afraid if I'm asked. That one breakthrough taught me not to fear but to trust and believe God can use me when he calls me.

God wants to use you to stand in the gap for others. But Satan knows if he can get you to cower in your fear, you'll never experience the breakthrough that comes when you face it. People you know and love will suffer as a result. I spent the first half of my life running from my fear instead of walking by faith. It's no way to live. I've learned firsthand that boldness precedes the miraculous. God miraculously transformed me and then used me to help others connect to Him, but it required boldness to face my fear. Only He could do something that amazing.

The good news is, He wants to do the same with you.

# CHAPTER 16

# TAKE ME TO THE WOODSHED

S peaking of fear and how Satan tries to use it to stifle the good works God has planned for His kids, we want to tell you about another incredible moment in our lives when God taught us a way to beat back fear.

Just after facing our fear from the "anti-gay" question from our producer before we signed with HGTV, we ran into another incident midway through filming when we had to face it again. Ugh! It's a part of our story we haven't told many people. It's about what happened when an activist group began pressuring HGTV to fire us.

We arrived on set that morning after praying the entire car ride over. We knew this attack against us was serious, and we needed all the help we could get. When we pulled up, the production crew was already in full motion, running around the house getting things ready. But we quickly noticed something unusual—something we hadn't seen on set before.

## POISED TO POUNCE

In an old beat-up car parked out front, a couple of girls sat staring us down, looking like they were going to jump out of the car and start a shout-down at any moment. They watched our every move as we parked and walked up to the set. We instantly knew these were protestors getting ready to stage some type of demonstration or disruption of the filming.

Now remember, this was after our "Peter moment" mentioned earlier when we were trying to save our show. We'd made it through that one, confessed, and ended up doing the right thing. Now we were being put to the test again. Fear came back in full force.

Seriously? That sucker is so hard to kill. But, herein lies the beauty of recognizing fear when it first raises its ugly head—it's the opportunity to be courageous. There's no such thing as courage without fear. Courage isn't the absence of fear—it's doing what's right in spite of it.

Here we were all over again, thinking, "We're going to lose the show, and people are going to hate us, and this stinks, and oh God please choose someone else." You know the feeling.

We really didn't want these girls to bring our whole production team into the drama. At this point, the crew had no clue about what was happening behind the scenes with HGTV—how they were being pressured to fire us. Fortunately, the girls drove off. We were pretty certain they were simply there to verify we actually had a show and were filming.

## FEAR'S EFFECTS

We both felt sick to our stomachs. It was clearly just a matter of time before the lid came off and protests started. The gut ache was bad. So bad we knew if we didn't get ourselves together it was going to negatively affect what we needed to do on camera that day. We didn't want to look like a couple of blundering idiots on reality television (although there are a few shows where that's worked out quite nicely for the network).

Isn't it interesting how fear can steal your confidence and cause you to go from feeling like a hero to a zero in the blink of an eye? For that brief moment walking up to the house, knowing full well we were being watched, both of us lost our mojo. Our shoulders were hunched, we weren't talking to anyone—all the joy we typically had on set was gone. Some of the very things that attracted HGTV to us vanished because of fear.

After we got our microphones on, I (Jason) motioned to David to follow me to the backyard. I knew from our past experience with fear the best way to overcome it was to get alone with God and pour our hearts out to Him. If we focused on the problem fear would *grow*, but if we focused on the Person (God) fear would *go*.

After turning our mics off, we walked behind a little grey shed out back, got down on our knees, and cried out to God. "Lord Jesus," we prayed. "We are afraid. We don't want to enter this fight because we know what they're going to do. They're coming after us for our values—for *Your* values. We could get seriously maligned and misrepresented by these people—and we don't want that. Our production company will get bullied and intimidated. HGTV may be picketed. Lord, we don't want this. Please take it away from us."

## THREE-STEP PRAYER

Taking a knee there outside, just out of earshot of the team supporting us, reminded us how it must have felt, at least in a very small way, for Jesus the night He was betrayed. We actually prayed the same prayer He prayed that night—"… Father! All things are possible for You; remove this cup from Me; yet not what I will, but what You will" (Mark 14:36). This three-step prayer has been something we have held onto for a long time and is extremely powerful when it comes to facing fear:

1. Recognize God's power—"All things are possible for You."
2. Request what you want or need—"Take this cup from Me."
3. Release it to God—"Yet not what I will, but what You will."

When we got to step one, we felt the stinging conviction that fear was still inside us and it needed to be dealt with. But the more we focused on the power of God, the smaller the problem we faced seemed. We could feel our faith taking over and winning the battle.

In the middle of praying, God spoke a verse into our hearts:

*One who is wise can go up against the city of the mighty and pull down the stronghold in which they trust.* (Proverbs 21:22)

At first it seemed out of place—what did this verse have to do with fear? But as we asked God for understanding, we heard Him say, "I'm about to put you in the public eye to deal with a spiritual stronghold that's capturing our nation, and you boys are there to tear it down. Have confidence in Me and do it."

We haven't had a lot of those, but that was a direct word from the Lord for us at that moment. Fear was growing fast, and God needed to give us courageous faith to overcome it. He did it by bringing clarity to what His plan was for us. We knew then we could faithfully release this entire thing into His sovereign hands.

## FEAR LOSES THE FIGHT

We walked behind the shed full of the Spirit (as all believers are), but we walked away from the shed in the power of the Spirit. We got "plugged-in" to God and we could feel His power flowing through us. Things were certainly moving in an unexpected direction, and the details of how it was all going to work out were still foggy, but God gave us clarity on our new assignment.

This all took place five days before we were fired. We tell people it was "divine sabotage." God gave us that show not so we could be on reality TV, but so we could be put in the middle of a cultural battle. And that's exactly what eventually happened.

We finished that day of filming with a new sense of purpose and gusto. It was a victory for us—we had confidence and joy. A spirit of fear would not control us. The apostle John said it this way, "*And this is the victory that has overcome the world: our faith*" (1 John 5:4). That fearful, downtrodden spirit was gone, and we were back to our old selves again. We weren't overly excited about the conflict we felt God was leading us straight into, but we accepted it without fear.

Looking back, we can see the importance of that prayer behind the shed. It was a pivotal time, preparing us for what lay ahead. We can see now the Lord was calling us to stand in the gap for that moment of time in our culture. This was right at the time when marriage was being redefined and religious liberty was under attack. But what did that have to do with us? We didn't want to lose our show or deal with the false perceptions that might come our way if we took a stand. So, we felt paralyzed, like bystanders on the sidelines watching our show drop into the toilet.

For a brief moment, we lost our focus. We stared intently at the thing God put in our hand—the platform of a prime-time reality show—and imagined the increase of our image, influence, and income. That possibility was clearly being threatened. So, our natural reaction was fear to protect what we had. Like Saul, we hoped hiding "in a tent from Goliath" would protect us until he went away. But God wanted us to operate in faith—like David, whose courage gave him the confidence to stand against a giant.

Those next several days of filming were a blur. And sure enough, five days later, our show was canceled. Yet in the midst of it all, we were able to overcome fear and operate confidently by faith whatever the cost.

Here's the funny part—to this date, years later, people still thank us for not being afraid to stand in the gap for truth. Not afraid? Are you kidding? We were afraid the whole time—we just chose not to be controlled by it. The Holy Spirit filled us with supernatural faith, which overcame our natural fears. There wasn't an interview we did where we weren't nervous or scared. We found ourselves plenty of times on our knees in a back room or closet somewhere praying and asking God for courage. Each time, He strengthened us to walk by faith and not by fear.

What we learned is being bold in faith doesn't always have to be dramatic, like David taking out Goliath or Peter preaching to thousands. Sometimes it's as simple as taking a knee when you're fearful, acknowledging his power, and handing the outcome back to him. Maybe it's saying, "God bless you" to the grocery store bagger, leaving a large tip with "Jesus loves you" on the receipt at the diner, or even refusing to let fear about your finances keep you from enjoying time with your family. Whatever it is, faith is simply choosing not to let fear take control. Refusing to let fear win and instead acknowledging Who has already won the ultimate battle for our lives.

You'll know it's time for you to stand in the gap because of the fear that comes along with it. Don't let it stop you from confidently doing what God calls you to do, no matter how small a task. Fear is the greatest enemy of faith, and faith—supernatural, bold faith—is exactly what it takes to bring heaven to earth.

## CHAPTER 17

# STOP! DON'T SHOOT!

The first time we met Nick Vujicic, we were in Washington, DC, at a pro-life gala listening to a full line-up of celebrity speakers. One after the other, they waxed eloquently, some making us laugh, some making us think, and even some making us cry (David: Actually, it was Jason who was crying). But when Nick came rolling out in a wheelchair with no arms and no legs, saying, "How can a man with no arms and no legs be the hands and feet of Jesus?" we were mesmerized. He had nothing—no limbs at all. His incredible confidence and authority took us back when he spoke. How could a dude with no arms and legs be such a complete person and speak with such authority? For the next ten minutes, we witnessed one of the most powerful, compelling, Spirit-filled men we've heard use his voice to bring heaven to earth.

Normally, we're not "stand in line" kind of guys at events, but this night was different for us. The minute the event was over, we instinctively rushed to the stage to meet Nick. On our way, we thought, "How are we going to shake his hand?" But not an instant after that thought popped into our heads, he looked up at us and said, "Bring it in for a hug, boys!"

Just like that, we were instantly "boys"—like BFFs. As soon as we hugged him, we felt an immediate bond of brotherhood. He wanted what we wanted—a mighty move of Jesus Christ in our generation. His eyes blazed with fire as he talked about his desire to see God move powerfully throughout the world and how he wanted to equip believers to be the hands and feet of Jesus in real, tangible ways. Then he said, "Give me your numbers, and let's keep in touch."

*Uh, how are you going to do that?* we thought to ourselves. Then out from under his left hip, he slid out his phone using a small appendage with two digits. He punched in our numbers and fired us off a text—it was amazing. Nick joked about it from the stage, "When people say, 'Give me a high-five,' I respond, 'How about a low-two?'"

A few months later, Nick came to Charlotte to preach a six-day evangelistic outreach. We attended the second night with great anticipation. Our kids and all the friends and acquaintances we could gather came with us. Nick absolutely crushed it. He concluded his message by saying, "God told me there are seventy people who will get saved tonight, and I'm not leaving until you come up to this altar. Now move!" We never heard an altar call quite like that before.

Just like that, seventy people came walking up. He counted them out loud as they came forward, which revealed he had way more faith than us. Sticking your neck out there when God clearly says something to you is scary business. One of our sons even rededicated his life to the Lord that night, which strengthened our bond with Nick all the more. But not until the next day did we really get to know Nick like we do now. The dude is straight up crazy (in a good way).

We invited him over for lunch and the first thing he said was, "One of you boys pick me up and put me in that chair over there." I (David) then grabbed him bear hug style and set him on Jason's patio chair. I didn't want to drop him, so I felt like I was squeezing him to death. Then he asked me to take off his shirt. Do what?! "I'm from California, bro, and when it's hot I lose the shirt." So I obliged, and when I did I was blown away with how fit this guy was. I mean, he's so hardcore, he even pays attention to his diet! After the shirt came off, away we went, talking about everything under the sun. We laughed, prayed, ate, and laughed some more. Our hearts were knit tight.

Jason and I were amazed at how grateful, humble, and confident Nick was. We know thousands of people, ourselves included at times, who don't possess these qualities to the level Nick does—and we have our arms and legs! To him, there's just no excuse to not be filled with joy. We loved it when he said, "If your circumstance can't change then your heart must."

We eventually told him about the concept of this book and asked if he'd share some of his story with us. He jumped right in and began to share:

## NICK'S STORY

I was born in Melbourne, Australia, with a rare genetic disorder called tetra-amelia syndrome (also known as phocomelia), which causes a child to be born with no arms or legs. If you want to know how special I am, only seven people in the world share the syndrome.

Believe me, I'm blessed.

Despite being bullied in school and feeling absolutely worthless early in life, by age fifteen, God grabbed my heart, gave me purpose and then began using me. I gave my life to Jesus Christ after reading John, Chapter 9 (healing of the man born blind).

When I was seventeen years old, the janitor of my high school said to me, "Nick, you're going to be a speaker." Wow. That felt good—this man believed in me. He then arranged for me to speak in front of six students at our public school's Bible Club. Talk about being a bridge for a disabled teenager! When I spoke, people started crying every time. I could tell God was using me to reach people. I thank God this man stood in the gap for me and made this opportunity happen.

Between the ages of seventeen and nineteen years, I began speaking more, also went into real estate and stock market investing, and graduated from Griffith University with a double degree in accounting and financial planning. Go big or go home, baby! (Jason: I feel like such an underachiever right now.)

Then, at the age of twenty-four years, I was in California, speaking in front of a congregation, and a man held up a little boy with no arms or legs. He was nineteen-month-old Daniel Martinez. I was blown away—he was just like me. So, I called for him to be brought up on stage, and I looked at him and had flashbacks of all the times when I was bullied and teased in elementary school, to the point of attempting suicide at age ten years. I realized, wow, man, if I went through all that just to help this kid, it's all been worth it. I could help him know God has a plan for him, that his disability is a blessing, not a burden, and he too could be the hands and feet of Jesus.

A few years later, when Daniel was getting teased in elementary school, his parents asked if I would go to his school and speak. Of course, I will! I did a fifteen-minute speech about loving yourself and loving everyone, and all of a sudden, he became the coolest kid in the school.

All worth it.

To this day, I've gone from school cafeterias and small churches to speaking in front of ten governments, eighteen presidents, and millions of people. I've had so many moments when God used a man like me, who the world might think has nothing to offer, to become a bridge that connects heaven to earth. But it hasn't always been easy.

I've discovered that to be a bridge God can use, as the Benham brothers discuss in this book, you will have to stare fear in the face and refuse to back down. In April 2017, I had to do just that.

I was asked to speak to the Ukraine government about legislation for the disabled. The country historically undervalued and overlooked the special-needs community. With all eyes on me and cameras capturing the moment, I spoke for twenty minutes about the Bible. Then I felt God tell me to ask them to get on their knees and pray. (David: Ha! Can you imagine that in America?!) One by one they began dropping to their knees. It's pretty amazing to witness governing leaders humble themselves like that. Then I prayed, according to 2 Chronicles 7:14, asking God's forgiveness for ignoring those with special needs so He'd heal their land and give them wisdom and strength to guide the country. Three weeks later they introduced a law to allow special-needs children to go to school for the first time.

I heard later my speech was broadcast over live television to twenty million Ukrainians and became the most-watched ninety minutes of Ukrainian television in five years.

The leaders asked me to come back later that year to gather with representatives of many denominations, Anglicans, Seventh-day Adventists, Baptists, Lutherans, Methodists, Mennonites, Presbyterians, and Charismatic Christians—all united to celebrate the 500th anniversary of the Protestant Reformation. It was a miracle just seeing all the denominations agree on something.

The Las Vegas shooting wouldn't happen until three weeks later, yet concerns over safety in public gatherings, because we were all sitting ducks with so many windows facing the streets, was very real—especially on this historic holiday. This was a massive public platform, and here I was in a foreign country, with who knows what out there. A sense of dread and fear overcame me like never before.

Six hours before the speech, I found myself crying on the phone with my wife. I said, "Baby, this could be it. There are 600 windows looking at me. I just feel it could be so easy for someone to take me out. Babe, I just want to say possibly goodbye, and if I go, I'll see you soon." That's what I was dealing with before that event. All this fear from Satan trying to get me to back down from what God called me to do. I've never felt fear like that before. But I drew strength from the Lord in that desperate moment.

Police would be there, sure, but what gave me most comfort was that we had 100 people constantly in prayer, the whole time, from morning to night. They walked those streets for a great many days, praying and fasting, right where nearly a million people would stand just days later. That was our best security measure, but still, they recommended I wear a bulletproof vest before taking the stage. Yet God had given me a new-found sense of courage, so I refused.

I just took a deep breath and rolled out on the stage, and the power of God came upon me in a mighty way. There were people as far as my eyes could see—an estimated 800,000 people were packed in those streets, and 400,000 of them gave their lives to Jesus Christ! In addition, twenty-six countries watched live without advertising interruption, and it was translated into twenty languages. They believe 52.7 million people heard the gospel of Jesus Christ. And I didn't get shot! I'm so thankful I didn't let fear control me but stepped out in faith and became a bridge that day for nearly a half million souls.

Here's something else amazing from that night. Nothing bad happened at all. I mean not one incident. In a stadium event, with 10,000 or 5,000 or even 500 people attending, emergencies come up all the time, like someone fainting or something. But I heard there were zero accounts of anything going wrong during that Ukrainian rally. I was worried about my life, but God took care of all the lives who were there, not just mine.

Had I not been on that stage because of my fear, I would not have seen 400,000 people give their lives to Jesus Christ. Now we're looking ahead, working to do more events like that, one in the Balkan region, one in Africa, and one in Latin America. Two hundred to 300 million people could watch on live TV all at the same time, moving us toward the goal of reaching one billion people in three events over the next seven years.

The more faith you have, the stronger you can become—you just have to step out. Because we grow today, we can move mountains tomorrow. Even a man without arms and legs can be the hands and feet of Jesus to get His work done.

By the way, I still communicate with my young friend, Daniel Martinez. As of the publication of this book, he's in middle school, around the Long Beach area. Recently, I got a call saying, "Nick, can you come to his school?"

I said, "Why? Is he getting teased?"

They said, "No." He's the president of the middle school, he's just told everybody about you, and they all want to meet you."

Big crowds or small, I can always be used by God to connect heaven with earth. Daniel is doing the same, and so can you.

# CHAPTER 18

# HOPE FOR THE HOPELESS

The whole time Nick was telling us his story in Jason's backyard, we were eating submarine sandwiches like we all just got out of prison. The three of us were mauling those bad boys. But how does a man with no arms and no legs eat subs with us like that? Well, that's where Peter Tafolla comes in.

When Jesus said the greatest among you must be the servant of all, we got to see a picture of what that actually looked like in Nick's caregiver, Peter. He looked more like a cage fighter than a caregiver, with huge shoulders, an edgy beard, and a look on his face that whispered, "you know I could crush you if I wanted to." Yet the minute he opened his mouth and started talking, all our fear disappeared.

Peter had been Nick's caregiver for a long time. They were a team, like a well-greased machine. Peter knew exactly what Nick would need or want before Nick would say a word. It was fun to watch. And he served with such tenderness and love too. It was a beautiful picture of Christ-like servant leadership.

Yet the coolest part of Peter's life was not that he was Nick Vujicic's caregiver, which is awesome on its own, but he and his wife have been foster parents to many kids in desperate situations and have even adopted some as their own.

As soon as we found out that little tidbit, we started pressing in for more of his story. We thought to ourselves, *Who is this guy that's feeding Nick bites of a sandwich (huge bites at that!) and traveling with him all over the world—and yet he has time to foster and adopt multiple children in desperate situations?*

Nick saw we were intrigued, so he told Peter to tell us his story. "You boys are going to love this!" Nick said. So Peter started in ...

## PETER'S STORY

My wife and I were devastated after we miscarried our first child and were told we could no longer have children. The pain was intense, but we knew with God's help we could turn the pain into a promise—for other children who didn't have parents.

So, we looked into adoption and realized that fostering was the best step toward adopting in our state (California). Almost immediately, after we finished the home study and completed the approval process, we got a call from a social worker saying there was a nine-month-old girl in need of care.

Oh boy! Here we go.

She told us this girl would be a lock for adoption and that within six to eight months she would be our legal daughter.

That was music to our ears!

"Alright, let's do this," we replied. And off we went to buy a crib, bottles, and clothes—this was our baby!

As my wife was signing all the paperwork the social worker said to us, "Hey listen, we have a surprise for you. She comes with a sister."

What?! We weren't expecting that. Our hearts leaped in our chests, but not from joy—it was fear.

"We know you guys didn't sign up for this," she continued, "but would you be able to at least host the little sister for a couple of days until we're able to find a place for her."

Now, what are we supposed to say to that?

Without further hesitation we agreed to help—we didn't want to talk ourselves out of it if we thought too much about it. We just knew we couldn't let this baby be left to the system.

But there was another catch; the sister was a newborn—like brand new newborn, perhaps twenty-four hours old. And she was premature and as light as a feather, weighing in at six and a half pounds.

This was an entirely new ballgame now.

We went to the hospital and brought her home, along with her big sister, and for the next forty-eight hours, all she did was scream and cry. When we changed her, her little feet would kick and kick, then stop, then kick and kick again. And she shivered the whole time. It was heart-wrenching. So we took her back to the hospital and found out, to our surprise, she was a crystal meth baby. Our hearts broke for this innocent little one, and for her sister. We felt such love for both of them.

Then, after several months, their great-grandmother called us out of nowhere and said she wanted both girls. We were in the church parking lot when we got the call from the social worker. Both of us fell to our knees and cried. We had fallen in love with these girls over the months—the thought of letting them go was gut-wrenching!

At that time, I really battled with God. How could He take these girls away from us after all we invested? We were completely broken.

After the grandmother took them away, we decided we were out of foster care for good. No more brokenness for us.

But God had other plans because a week and a half later I got another phone call. The social worker on the other end said, "I know you guys don't want to hear from us right now, but we have three sisters who need a temporary place to stay. Can you help us out?"

Automatically my heart said, no way. We're not going through that kind of heartache again. Losing our two girls was more than we could bear. We wanted to focus on our marriage instead.

But the worker went on. "There are no beds available for these three girls," she said. "It's an emergency situation. I promise they will be out of your life by Monday."

So, I called my wife back and gave her the rundown. "Pete," she responded, "we just came out of this crazy week and a half being emotional, crying, and broken." Then she paused. I wasn't sure what she'd say next. To my surprise, she said, "You know what—it's only three days. What could it hurt?"

To be honest, we were afraid. Foster care forces you into situations where you fall in love with these kids, see them in your homes, begin to imagine a future with them, and then suddenly they're torn out of your lives. But despite our hesitation, we strongly felt God wanted us to help one more time.

The three sisters showed up at our house later that day—a twelve-year-old, a four-year-old, and a two-year-old. Beautiful Hispanic girls with long, flowing dark hair. We immediately fell in love with them. The twelve-year-old was tall. The four-year-old was a little chubby, adorable, and always wanting to be picked up and held. The two-year-old had big, beautiful eyes, but she didn't speak and always cried. We couldn't imagine the emotional pain she must've been experiencing.

So we decided to have a little welcome dinner that night to make them feel comfortable and loved. After dinner, I asked if we could take a picture, and what the little four-year-old girl did next shook me to the core.

She said to me, "Sure—we can take a picture. Gimme one minute." She then went into the bathroom and came back out in her underwear, saying, "I'm ready for my picture."

My wife and I were horrified. What on earth has this child been through?!

Then her twelve-year-old sister told us the story of what happened five hours before they arrived—they were rescued out of a child pornography ring. Here was this little twelve-year-old girl, who should've been playing with friends and enjoying her childhood, describing to us every gross detail you can think of that one man was doing to her sisters while she had to watch. It turns out the guy had one of the biggest child pornography rings in the San Fernando Valley, selling child pornography out of his home. He was the adult son of a babysitter in the area. His mom had no idea he was doing this to the children.

The twelve-year-old said, "This is why my sister took off her clothes. She understands pictures as 'picture time.'" We couldn't keep the emotions in any longer. We sat there bawling our eyes out. Now we understood why this two-year-old girl didn't speak. Her little mind was traumatized. We called the social workers, who said they knew about the situation (failing to tell us first), and the authorities arrested the guy.

Right then I felt the Lord say to me, "I am calling you and your wife to be a father and a mother to those who don't have fathers and mothers in their lives." It completely broke me.

Later, after the girls went to sleep, I told my wife what I felt the Lord said, and she agreed. "Pete," she said in her calm, don't-wake-the-kids voice, "I feel the same thing. I believe this is what God is calling us into."

We called the social workers and told them there was no rush finding another foster home for the girls. We ended up hosting them for about eleven months. During that time, we were able to talk to them about Jesus, pray with them, even help the twelve-year-old through a confusing time of gender identity, which eventually led to her giving her life to Christ at a church camp.

Even after all that the older sister went through, she taught us about grace and mercy. The case against the child pornographer was going to trial, and the prosecutors wanted her to testify about what she saw. There weren't any witnesses old enough who could be credible on the witness stand. They had disgusting videos, but the guy's face wasn't in them. She was the only way he could go to jail because she saw what he did with her own eyes.

Around this time, she and I were getting ice cream together, and she said, "Hey, Papa Pete, can I ask a question? What do you think is going to happen to this guy if he goes to jail?" I gave her a very straight up answer. "Honestly honey, a lot of things can happen to this guy. Men like him do not get treated with respect in prison. In prison, guys like him will experience some pretty hard stuff by the other prisoners."

I could see her thinking intently about what I just told her. Then she looked up at me and said, "Papa Pete, I'm ready to talk about what he did, but can we pray for him? For God's mercy on him. For God to forgive him and for him to find Jesus." Then she prayed the most amazing prayer for this man so he would find God's mercy and have His protection while in jail.

I have never witnessed such unconditional love like that in my life.

Two and a half years later, now adopted by their aunt, I got a phone call from the oldest daughter. "I just wanted to call and say thank you," she said in that familiar little voice. "Thank you for introducing me to Jesus. Thank you for praying for me. Thank you for giving me my Bible. My friends think that I'm a Jesus freak because I talk to them about Jesus in my school."

Her words warmed our hearts. We knew we had walked in obedience to God, and it had a profound impact on these three young girls.

Fostering those girls was an emotionally hard time for us, but we would never have traded it for anything. Since that time, my wife and I have had the pleasure of fostering more than twenty-five children, and we actually adopted one little boy who came into our home at three months old. It took 790 days for his adoption to be final—but we got him. Praise the Lord!

Fear—selfish, protective fear—almost kept us from being a bridge of grace for these kids. Foster care and adoption are scary things because you put all of yourself out there, all your emotions and resources on the line, and to be honest, you get hurt. You get crushed.

But that's what servants of the Lord do—we act like Christ and are willing to take the crushing to bring hope to the hopeless. If Christians get involved in the foster care and the adoption system, we have a chance to show these kids—these abused, forgotten, discarded kids—a God who will never hurt them, forget them, or forsake them. For me, that's what being a bridge is all about.

God calls us His adopted children. He sacrifices everything for us. He invests and risks His heart on us. We can do this for others too.

# CHAPTER 19

# BOLD FAITH

One of our favorite family movies of all time is *War Room*, by Alex and Stephen Kendrick. Our kids often ask us to play it when we're on road trips, and we gladly oblige because it's an inspiring film that shows the power and importance of prayer, which is vital in the life of every believer who chooses to stand in the gap for God.

In the movie, an older woman, Miss Clara, teaches a struggling wife how to pray—how to create a war room of prayer where she does battle on her knees against the spiritual forces of darkness, especially those tearing her marriage apart. The final scene ends with Miss Clara in her own war room—a small closet in her house—on her knees crying out to God to raise up a generation of believers who will do battle for the Lord.

"Raise 'em up, Lord, raise 'em up!" Miss Clara prayed. "Raise up warriors, Lord, who will fight on their knees!"

If you haven't seen the movie you should. There's no doubt it will energize your prayer life. Your kids will love it too, and the prayer at the end will blow your hair back.

## *WAR ROOM* IN OUR OWN BACKYARD

Interestingly, the movie was filmed in our hometown, Concord, North Carolina. We've been friends with the Kendrick brothers for years, so when they were looking for a place to film their next movie, we pitched the idea of filming it here. Well, maybe we didn't pitch the idea as much as we threatened them—"You'll film the movie here or we will punch you both in the face." Just kidding! But they did eventually cave and brought the entire movie production here in the summer of 2014.

But a movie on prayer filmed in our hometown meant more to us than anyone involved ever really knew. We moved to Concord in the early 2000s just after professional baseball because of a man who had his own war room—a man who changed the direction of our lives forever. He lived out the *War Room* life, especially the final scene where Miss Clara was on her knees crying out to God. That scene was an exact picture of what this man did every single morning, in Concord, just a few miles from where Miss Clara's prayer scene was filmed. Never before had we seen a man of prayer quite like him, nor had we been around someone who fought God's battles on his knees with such spiritual power and tenacity.

## FLASHBACK TO COLLEGE DAYS

We met this prayer warrior in the Fall of 1997. We were juniors at Liberty University, and we spent Thanksgiving in Atlanta, Georgia, with all our extended family. We spent four straight days indulging our appetites for both food and football. We consoled ourselves by saying we were simply working on our "before pictures" for our New Years fitness resolutions.

While we were in Atlanta, our dad told us he wanted us to meet this real estate tycoon who was doing amazing things for the Lord in Concord.

"His name is David Drye," he said. "He flew me in to speak to his company and the school and be on his show."

Evidently, this guy was a successful businessman who started a Christian school and hosted a Christian television show. Mr. Drye lived in Concord, which just happened to be on our way back from Atlanta to Liberty. When Dad told him we'd be passing through, he invited us to spend the night at his house on Sunday night and then speak to his team on Monday morning.

We showed up that Sunday night and quickly realized our dad seriously underplayed Mr. Drye's business success. From the enormity of his house and size of his property, it was clear he experienced a level of financial success beyond anything we ever saw. Our first thoughts were, "What kind of business does this guy have, and how can we get involved?"

We walked up the brick steps and were greeted by a bright-smiling fifty-year-old man who beamed with excitement. "I'm so glad you guys are here," he said. "Come in and meet my family."

We had never been in a house quite like that in all our lives. By the time we stopped gasping at the magnitude of the place, we noticed in the living room a bunch of kids sitting on couches eating. They were the five youngest of his eight children.

"You guys want a Mr. C's burger?" he asked. "These things are famous around here."

Asking a couple starving college guys if they would like to eat burgers is like asking if fat puppies like big bones. Of course, they do! There's no need to ask.

After indulging in a few Mr. C's burgers and confirming they were worthy of the "famous" tag, we followed Mr. Drye upstairs to our room for the night. He put us in his boy's room, just down the hall from his office. We were bummed we had to take the stairs instead of the elevator—apparently, he wanted us to get a workout.

"Breakfast is at 7:00 A.M.," he said. "We've got a big day planned for tomorrow."

As we lay there in the darkened silence of that room, we quietly marveled at how successful this man was. We were raised by a preacher in a lower-middle-class family, and most Christians we knew were like us. We didn't run in circles with people like this guy.

We drifted off to sleep in the amazing comfort of beds that far exceeded our dorm room twin-sized mattresses back at Liberty. Then, at 4:30 A.M. we were startled awake by the sound of someone yelling down the hall.

## AWAKE AT DAWN

"Dude! What's that?" We both got up and crept to the door, cracked it open, and looked down the long dark hallway. We could see light coming out from under the door of Mr. Drye's office. As we stood there with bated breath and hearts pounding, we realized he wasn't yelling—he was praying.

For the next hour, we heard him pouring his heart out to the Lord and doing battle with the enemy. He would go from telling God how much he loved Him to rebuking the devil in the name of Jesus. "You have no authority over my family or my business, devil!" he shouted. "Get away from them!"

We grew up in a family that believed in prayer and put that belief into practice. But this was a whole new level—never before had we seen such emphatic prayer. This man was on his knees in hand-to-hand combat with the devil.

Fortunately, we were able to fall back asleep for about an hour. The next time we woke up was more pleasant—the smell of eggs and bacon beckoned to us from downstairs. There's nothing like the aroma of bacon in the morning and the sizzling it makes as it fries in the pan. We slid downstairs in a food trance.

## TESTIMONY OVER BACON

David's wife, Ann, whipped up an amazing breakfast for us and for the rest of her tribe. We sat around the table as each kid filled the empty chairs, one by one.

"We heard you praying early this morning," we told Mr. Drye.

"Oh. Sorry about that," he said. "I go to war on my knees before I start my day or I don't feel right."

As we sat there with their family crushing Mrs. Ann's amazing cooking, Mr. Drye told us the story behind their eight kids. After he and his
wife had their first three, they decided they were done. But then God
began to convict them to have more. This was right at the time he started
his own business, so it was a scary thought. In response to God's prompting, Mr. Drye made a deal with God.

"Lord," Mr. Drye said, "If you want us to have more kids we'll do
it. But I pray that you'll make us richer with every kid we have."

They had five more. And as far as we could, tell God answered that
prayer—in a BIG way.

We polished off breakfast and were whisked away in his Suburban
to his office where we were set to speak to his staff. On the way, we asked
dozens of questions about how he started the business.

## THE MISSION

"I began in insurance," he said. "But then I realized I wanted to create
something that could make millions of dollars to fund God's work on
the earth. So, I got into real estate."

Whoa. We had never heard anyone talk like that before. A person
who wanted to make millions of dollars to give away?

Before we could get the next question out of our mouths, we pulled
up to a big white building with "David Drye Company" on the marquee
sign out front. We walked into the foyer and up the stairs to a large
conference room where about thirty people were gathered, waiting for
Mr. Drye—and us.

*This guy has thirty employees?* we thought. *That's huge!* We quickly
found out these people were only a few of his leaders and support staff.
His company had nearly 400 employees who managed forty-three apartment complexes across two states.

We spent the whole day with him as he hauled us from one speaking
engagement to the next. The longer we were with him, the more
impressed and inspired we became. We probably asked him no fewer

than 100 questions. We couldn't drive more than two or three miles without him pointing out another apartment complex he owned, or a fun-park he opened, or office complex he built. And the whole time, he explained that his entire business was built upon prayer.

"I have prayed for the last twenty years that God would bless my business," he said. "I shout, 'God, bust those rocks and break those chains that hold back your blessing from me. I commit my way to you. Give me more that I may bless you with it!' Boys, God has answered my prayers."

While he was talking, his fists were balled up and swinging wildly. He was a pretty passionate guy. And he had no idea how to wait until his truck came to a complete stop before he changed gears. He'd back out of a parking spot at warp speed and slam it into drive before he even pushed the break. It was an adventurous ride that day.

At the end of the day as we were driving back to his house, he asked if we would mind flying back to Liberty in his helicopter since he didn't have time to drive us back.

"Uh, are you kidding?" we thought. "That would be amazing!" We had never been in a helicopter before.

When we pulled onto his half mile long driveway at his house he reached in his pocket and pulled out a small, worn piece of paper. "Do you boys know what this is," he asked.

"No sir," we said.

"On this sheet of paper," he continued, "I've written goals for my family and my business. When you guys heard me this morning I was laying my hands on these goals and asking God to help me accomplish everything on the list. But I know Satan doesn't want me to succeed, so when I pray I know I've entered a battlefield in the spiritual realm. I wage war in the spirit before I go to war in business."

As he was talking, he handed us the piece of paper. "Take a look," he said. "I want you to see what I've written on there. I don't usually do this, but I feel the Lord wants me to let you see."

We couldn't get past the first two points:

1. Give away $1 million a month from my business.
2. Bring home $100,000 a month for my family.

We had never seen numbers like that before, much less written on a piece of paper and prayed over by a man who was well on his way to accomplishing it (if he hadn't already). He handed it to a couple broke college kids who barely knew how they were going to fill their truck with gas. But the Lord told him to show it to us. We're glad he did. What stuck out most was his first goal revealed the amount he wanted to give away—90%.

He looked at us with penetrating eyes. "Boys, I believe God has a great plan for both of you," he said. "But that plan is only going to go as far as your prayer life is deep. You need to go after God in prayer like never before. Make big goals for yourselves spiritually and financially and then go after them until He either grants your request or changes what you should ask for."

When we gave the paper back to him, he asked us something that changed the trajectory of our lives. "When baseball is over," he said, "would you consider coming to work for me, so I can teach you what I know? I've been praying for God to spark a revival in America right here from Concord, and I want to pour myself into young men like you."

Uh, do bears poop in the woods? We responded with an emphatic "Yes!" David Drye gave us a vision for life after baseball. To be part of a thriving business led by a man with a heart to change the world for Christ—now *that* was magnetizing.

Just before we left, he opened the tailgate of his suburban, reached his hand into one of the several boxes inside, and handed us each a copy of the autobiography of George Mueller. "Aside from the Bible, this is the best book I've ever read," he told us. "I give them out to everyone I can. I have modeled my prayer life after this great man, and you should too."

Inside each book was his business card. The front of the card just said "Jesus Loves You" in big red letters. On the back was his contact information. It was a simple way to let people know what was most important in his life.

We prayed together and then said goodbye.

Our heads were buzzing on the flight back to Liberty, not just because we were stoked to be flying in a helicopter but because we felt this could be one of the most life-changing days of our lives. We had no idea what the future held, but finally, we had a vision for life after baseball and a powerful prayer life to go with it.

The pilot landed in the outfield of our baseball stadium. Talk about the best thing that could happen to a couple college athletes—we looked like big wigs getting off that thing and running with our heads down. It was like a scene from a movie.

## THE IMPACT

Our prayer lives changed that day. From that point forward, we began to pray bold prayers like we never prayed before, recognizing prayer is a battle and we are to wage war on our knees. We also read the book. If you haven't read about the life of George Mueller, it's a must-read. Put it on your list. It's in our top five books of all time.

A year later, we were both drafted into professional baseball—David by the Red Sox and me (Jason) by the Orioles. In my second year as a minor leaguer for the Orioles, I broke my leg in Hickory, North Carolina. We tell the story in detail in our book *Miracle in Shreveport*. It was an epic break, one that required emergency surgery and several days in the hospital.

Because it was the final game of a seven-day road trip, our team couldn't wait for me, so they left me behind and headed home. By the time I got out of surgery, I was stuck by myself in Hickory, alone in a hospital room.

The next morning, after I finished breakfast, I heard a knock at the door. "Come in," I said, wondering who in the world it could be. Low and behold, and to my total amazement, it was David Drye and one of his sons. We hadn't seen each other in two years.

"We heard about what happened to you and we came to pray for your healing," he said with a huge smile on his face. "You didn't think you could be so close to us and I wouldn't come see you, did you?" Hickory was less than an hour from Concord.

"How did you hear?" I asked.

"Your dad called last night to ask for prayer," he said. "So I told him I would do even better—I'd come pray for you in person."

I was so thankful to see a familiar face. I was even more thankful it was a man who prayed like him.

As we were talking together, he gave out his "Jesus Loves You" business card to every nurse or doctor who came into the room. Then he placed one in the picture frame on the wall in front of my bed. I looked at that thing every day I was in the hospital.

After we prayed together, I said, "I just gotta ask—did you fly your helicopter here?"

He smiled big. "Yep. Landed it on the roof."

He then asked if I read the book on George Mueller. I told him I did and how it definitely lived up to the hype. He said he'd send me a case full of them so I could give them to the guys on my team.

He then reminded me that he wanted David and me to come work with him when baseball was over. "That's a deal," I said.

He leaned over and hugged me in bed. When he walked out of the room, I was struck with the feeling that this was one of the greatest human beings I met in my life. I remember thinking it would be nice to be like him one day.

One month later, I was recovering in Dallas at my parents' house when we got a phone call.

"David Drye and his wife Ann were just killed in a plane crash," the voice on the other line said.

I lost my breath.

They were on his private plane headed to their beach house when one of the engines failed. The pilot almost made it back to the runway, but their wing clipped a tree and the plane flipped upside down. The pilot, David and Ann, and one of their senior leaders were all killed.

I couldn't believe what I heard. "There's no way—just no way he's gone," I thought. My mind was racing a million directions. I put so much hope into a future with Mr. Drye, and he was gone. "His family. His business. Lord help them," I prayed.

Two days later and still in shock from that phone call I received, a package arrived from Concord. I opened it, and there was the case of George Mueller books Mr. Drye promised to send. On top was a scribbled note in his hand-writing:

"Have fun giving these out. Let's talk soon—David Drye"

He mailed that box to me before he boarded the plane that day. I could barely keep it together.

I placed one of the copies on my bookshelf, the same one I still have today. It serves as a constant reminder, not just of the prayer warrior the book is about but also of the prayer warrior who gave it to me.

## THE PERFECT PLACE TO LAUNCH OUR MISSION

Two years later in 2001, when baseball was all over for me, I took a job as the ministry coordinator for the David Drye Company. It was a position Mr. Drye created before his death with a two-fold purpose: to be a chaplain for the employees and outreach coordinator for the community.

Within two year's time, our entire Benham family relocated to Concord, in large part because of the doors the David Drye Company opened for us. When my brother got out of baseball the next year in 2002, he took a job as the janitor at David Drye's school. Our sister, Tracy, became the David Drye Company secretary, and our dad was part of the pro-life outreach the company supported. Even in death, David Drye's life brought divine connection for our family—helping establish the plan God had for us here on earth.

## CONNECTING HEAVEN TO EARTH

By the time 2014 rolled around and the Kendrick Brothers told us about their idea for making a movie about the power of prayer, we knew there was only one place it could be filmed—right where the embodiment of the message took his last breath. To us, *War Room* served as a tribute to the life David Drye.

There is a scene in the movie where Tony comes into a gym, sees his daughter jumping rope, and stands there as a proud daddy smiling in awe of what she can do. That scene was filmed in the gymnasium of the school David Drye founded and funded with his generous kingdom giving. Now his investment has been seen all over the world in a movie that itself is a testament of how God answered his prayers.

One of the most powerful ways to stand in the gap for others and for this nation is to pray. To pray like David Drye prayed. To fight your battles with bold faith in prayer, on your knees, asking God to "bust the rocks and break the chains" of the devil, to use you to connect heaven to earth in powerful, supernatural ways for your family and for those around you. Because you never know when you've lived your last day. The prayers you pray today just might pave someone else's path tomorrow.

## CHAPTER 20

# FLAWED AND FAITHFUL

Since we got the heave-ho from HGTV in 2014, we've done our fair share of media interviews—as in more than. When you get that much airtime, people tend to reduce you to a sort of "brand." Somehow, the two of us have gotten a bit of a reputation as the twin brothers—or "dynamic duo" as some have said—who are paragons of virtue. This makes us laugh out loud because nothing could be further from the truth, and honestly, "paragon" is a big word for us. (We had to look it up.)

First of all, if there is anything worthy of praise in our lives, it is only the work of Jesus Christ. Secondly, we're absolutely capable of sin—we're so fallible it's not funny. The good news is: Being super fallible puts us in good company. Over and over again, we've seen how God uses broken vessels, not perfect ones.

Just take a look at how God reveals the faults and sinful deeds of the men and women in Scripture. He didn't use perfect people; He used broken people—those marred by sin but forgiven by God. Abraham was a liar. Jacob was a deceiver. Aaron was an idolater. Rahab was a prostitute. David was an adulterer. Paul was a murderer. The list goes on. The Bible hides nothing about the men and women God used to bring heaven to earth in real ways. And the key to His use of them was not their *perfect*ness but their *broken*ness.

We love how Warren Wiersbe, one of our favorite Bible commentators, put it: "Every great personality mentioned in the Bible sinned at one time or another. Abraham lied about his wife (Gen. 12:10–20). Moses lost his temper and disobeyed God (Num. 20:7–13). Peter denied the Lord three times (Matt. 26:69–75). But sin was not the settled practice of these men. It was an *incident* in their lives, totally contrary to their normal habits. And when they sinned, they admitted it and asked God to forgive them."

This is what the faithful believers before us did. They were broken over their sin and submitted their selfish, stubborn ways to God. If we didn't get to see their raw, real-life *incidents* of sin, we'd all probably throw our hands up in despair and wonder how, or if, God could ever use us today. But God didn't do that to us; instead, He brought us into the darkest, most intimate secrets of their lives and showed how broken people can be restored *to* Him and then used *for* Him in powerful ways.

## OWNING OUR "WRETCHEDNESS"

Every time we sing "Amazing Grace," we love how spot-on the third line is: "that saved a *wretch* like me." John Newton wrote the song in 1779. He was a slave trader who came to faith and repented of his sins, penning this song in the glorious days after his conversion. Some contemporary versions of the song omit this line, perhaps because this is where the rubber meets the road for many believers today. So many times, we conceal our sinfulness for fear of getting smeared by others and not being useful to God anymore. But God destroys shame in the light of truth. When we share our true selves honestly, we bring heaven to earth like nothing else. The power of our testimony—how we were broken, restored, and then used by God—stands as hope and mercy for others.

## GETTING REAL

I (David) will be the first to admit what a pathetic sinner I've been. I've lied, cheated, gossiped, stolen, and more. I've been hypocritical and judgmental. I've blessed God from one side of my mouth while cursing out the other. But I've grown in the Lord; those sinful ways are not part of my lifestyle anymore. As a young man, I had *habits* more than *incidents*, like struggles with deceit, lust, and anger. But as I've walked in God's light, the gentle heat of His presence has burned those habits away—like feeling heat the closer you get to a light source.

But as an older man, I still have incidents from time to time. We all do. Here are three I've struggled with over the years.

## CALM DOWN

The biggest issue in my adult life used to be losing my temper. When my kids were younger, I was so concerned about their being perfect that any misbehavior—foolish or willful—would be met with angry correction. I didn't shepherd their hearts beside the "still water" like the Good Shepherd, but, more like a mean shepherd, I led them to the "rushing torrent" of angry, verbal correction. Yet God broke me of this, and He used my youngest son to do it.

Our family was watching a prerelease movie with our friends the Kendricks. It's one of the fringe benefits we get for hanging out with them—they see all the newest faith-based releases before they hit theaters. There was a scene halfway through this movie where the dad yelled angrily at his son, then knocked over a table, and looked at his boy as though he wanted to hit him. It was hard to watch. When the scene ended, my youngest boy crawled onto my lap, and with his thumb in his mouth he looked at me and whispered, "Daddy, will you ever do that to me?"

I couldn't believe he asked me that question. I wondered, *Have I developed such a fear in my boy he actually thinks I may lose it on him like this guy? What a stinkin' wretch I am!*

My heart broke. Here was my son, sitting in my lap with his thumb in his mouth, looking at me with eyes longing, even begging, for me to assure him I would never do such a thing to him. Thankfully, I never did anything like that before, but the sheer fact he asked meant I had already damaged his little heart.

I wrapped him in my arms tighter than ever, and with tears in my eyes, I promised him—from the bottom of my heart—I would never do that to him. I also begged him to forgive me for making him feel that way. God literally broke me with one simple question from my son.

I told my wife what he said, and over the next few days, she helped me see even more clearly what anger can do to a child's heart. I finally saw the light. I asked God to forgive me and then pulled all my kids into the living room to repent. I asked for their forgiveness and committed to fully submit to God in that area of my life. Today, I'm a broken father, fully restored and able to lead much better.

## AMBITION IN THE WRONG SEAT

Just about the time I got my anger under control, I realized I needed to do the same with my ambition. Jason and I are entrepreneurs, which means we know how to make things happen and move stuff forward. We have discovered, however, that ambition is an entrepreneur's best friend—so long as it stays in the passenger seat. The minute it jumps in the driver's seat, you'll end up going the wrong way.

I saw this up close my first few months as a real estate agent. I put together a deal on four houses that would allow me to make a good amount of money outside of closing. This meant a certain portion of money would change hands but not be disclosed to the closing attorney. At first, I didn't know it was wrong because I was new in the industry and lots of other agents did it. But after I found out, I still tried to push the deal through. We desperately needed the money, so I rationalized that it wouldn't be a big deal. Besides, if other agents did it, then it can't be that bad. But it was still wrong—and I knew it.

I told Jason about the deal, and he questioned me. "Are you sure we're supposed to do that?" he said. "We'll be fine," I told him, "Besides, there's nothing *really* wrong here because everyone involved is fully aware of what's going on."

Uh, that didn't matter—because it was wrong. Thankfully, God used my broker in charge to show me the error of my ways.

"Guys. Any time you overstate a price and try to get money outside of closing, it's illegal," he said. "You boys are going to make enough money in real estate, just do it the right way."

I knew in my heart he was right. So, I pulled out of the deal, lost a little bit of money, and asked God to forgive me for letting my ambition take the lead. Years later, and with my conscience fully intact, my brother and I ended up building one of the fastest-growing private real estate franchises in America. Only God. I was broken of my selfish ambition and let God-honoring ambition—full of honesty—drive us to success.

## EMOTIONS IN THE WRONG SEAT

Although I learned to harness my ambition, I also had to learn to harness my emotions as well. Earlier in my marriage, I made sure all the doors of my heart were locked tight (from pornography, etc.), yet one time I failed to realize a small window that was cracked open. And God used my egghead brother to bring it up to me (ugh!). I didn't believe him at first—I was blind to it—because in my mind the major doors of my heart were closed. I didn't feel the draft from this "little" window at all.

I was always friendly with girls growing up, but truth be told I was more of a flirt, even into the early years of my marriage. I never would've admitted it back then, but I do now. I thank God He has restored me, and I have strong boundaries in place, but early on, I didn't have the checks in my life I do now. One time, in particular, I had become so comfortable with a girl I nearly fell into a full-blown affair. It wasn't a lustful thing but a familiar thing, a flirty thing that started out as a friendly thing, and it needed to stop before it turned into a fiery thing. Sorry for the alliteration—it just flowed. Hell's fire instead of heaven's freedom was singing my toes, and I didn't even feel it.

But God won the victory and provided a way out—He saved me from it, just like His word says, "No temptation has overtaken you except what is common to mankind. And God is faithful; He will not let you be tempted beyond what you can bear. But when you are tempted, *He will also provide a way out* so that you can endure it" (1 Corinthians 10:13, emphasis added).

Jason was God's way out for me because he sensed what was happening and stepped in with a fierce rebuke. It awakened me to the reality of what was truly going on, and I immediately stopped dead in my tracks. I told him, and then I told Lori and asked for forgiveness. I told my pastor, too, and a few other men who could hold me accountable. I repented to God and then slammed that window shut, tight—forever.

So many years have passed since then, and to this day, there remains a security and safety with God-honoring boundaries in my life more than I could have ever imagined. I continue to grow closer to the Lord and my wife, not as a perfect man but as a broken one, fully submitted to my King.

## HOW GOD USES BROKEN PEOPLE

Through my own struggles, I've seen firsthand how God uses broken people (over their sin) not perfect people (without sin).

Sin is a destroyer, but God is a restorer. Maybe you've been caught in sin's grip before. Maybe you didn't have a brother (or sister) to stand in the gap for you. Or perhaps you refused to listen, ended up walking further down sin's path, and have suffered greatly. Can God still use you? Or are you just to be left on the scrap heap of Christian history, ineffective for Him.

I have good news for you—God can and will use you if you let Him. Broken horses are useful horses. Our dad used to say, "Only the horses willing to be broken by the master are fit to pull the king's chariot. The rest are left to pasture." So, if you've confessed your sins and forsaken them, assuming full responsibility for your actions and accountability for future ones, then you are a broken person God can use in mighty ways. As a matter of fact, He can take your mess and make it a message and even a ministry—He's just that good.

But Satan wants you to stay trapped in fear, guilt, and shame. He doesn't want you to stand in the gap and do the will of God. He's an accuser, so whenever God wants to use you, Satan will be right there to whisper in your ear, reminding you of the "wretch" you once were (see Zechariah 3:1–5). But you have to speak the truth: God's amazing grace "saved a wretch like me!"

## BASELESS ACCUSATIONS

Several years ago, I felt the Lord leading Jason and me to spearhead a citywide prayer service for revival and awakening in Charlotte. That's when I heard the accusation for the first time, "You can't be used by God," followed by the memory of sins in the past—sins for which I had already been forgiven.

But God brought Psalm 66:18–19 to my mind. The man after God's own heart (David) said, "If I had cherished sin in my heart, the Lord would not have listened; but God has surely listened and has heard my prayer." So, I knew in my mind God would hear my prayers. I wasn't cherishing sin in my heart. I was fully submitted to His will and ways, but this voice kept coming back.

"You can't be used by God."

It was a real battle for me. I had no trouble leading in small ways, but a project of this magnitude felt more intense. Yet, as the accusations came with each passing day, the voice of the Lord in my spirit began to come even louder and more frequently.

"Gather My church for prayer."

The more I watched our nation decline spiritually and morally, the more I heard the urgency of the Lord's call. So, I spent dedicated time in prayer over it, asking God how He could use a guy like me.

Then I turned to Psalm 51 and read another prayer by David:

"Have mercy on me, O God, according to your unfailing love; according to your great compassion blot out my transgressions. Wash away all my iniquity and cleanse me from my sin … Restore to me the joy of your salvation and grant me a willing spirit, to sustain me. *Then I will teach transgressors your ways* so that sinners will turn back to you." (Psalm 51:1–4, 7–13).

Those verses spoke directly to me. After full repentance, confession of sin, and assumption of responsibility, God could use anyone—even me—to help others turn back to Him. He could use an old, broken horse like me to pull the chariot of His presence into our city.

Standing on that incredible promise I decided to join my brother and lead this prayer service. I was a broken man, just like King David, which is exactly the kind of person God could use to bring heaven to earth. More than 9,000 people poured into an amphitheater with more than 150 churches uniting to seek the Lord that day. It was truly a supernatural event. Years later, people still reach out to us saying how impactful that time was in their lives.

The Lord continues to work in my life, drawing me closer to Him with each passing day. My desire is to be useful for His kingdom, to be a Godly husband, father, and worker. And He does it every time I submit to Him.

If you find yourself asking if God could ever use you because of your past, go back and see if there's something left to confess. If so, confess it and seek reconciliation with those affected. Let God break you—He is always faithful to forgive and restore. But then—get ready, because He can and will use you—and quite possibly your sinful story—to connect heaven to earth for others in a powerful way.

# CHAPTER 21

# TELL ME YOUR STORY

There's an intimate story recorded in the Gospels that beautifully illustrates the transforming power of grace and the power of using our testimony of transformation. In it, we see one of those rare moments when Jesus wasn't in the middle of a huge crowd. Instead, he spoke kindly but truthfully to a hurting woman and transformed her life forever. How she responded to it is a model for all of us to follow if we're going to become a bridge connecting heaven to earth.

"The man you're living with isn't your husband."

Now *that's* quite a way to get someone's attention. This is what Jesus said mid-conversation to a woman he just met at a local well one afternoon outside Samaria.

Back in Bible times, the women went down to the well in the morning or evening when it was in the cool of the day. To be there in the middle of the day revealed this woman either had an emergency or was avoiding other women altogether. Her response proved the latter was most likely the case.

"I have no husband," she replied.

"You're right about that," Jesus responded. "For you have had five husbands, and the one whom you now have is not your husband" (John 4:16–18).

Good grief! Can you imagine talking like this to someone? It's no wonder she probably didn't want to be around the other ladies. She went through men like our dad goes through fudgesicles! (Sorry, Dad.)

But Jesus was going somewhere with her—and He had a plan. Little did she know what the future had in store for her and just how instrumental she would be for Jesus in connecting the people in her town back to God.

But first, Jesus had to work *in* her before He could work *through* her.

The fact Jesus was talking to her—both as a woman and as a Samaritan—proved He loved and cared for her even though He would assuredly be misunderstood. Hebrew men didn't talk with women openly in the street, and there was much animosity between Jews and Samaritans. But Jesus threw off these cultural norms because He sought to show grace and mercy to this woman—to stand personally in the gap for her.

She arrived at the well that day to get water, but Jesus was there to give her living water. That's what she truly needed—to reconnect with the God who created her by entering a relationship with His Son.

To do this, He had to first point out her sin—because if there is no sin, there is no need for a Savior. He wasn't there to simply point this out to her and make her feel guilty—He was there to give her the hope of eternity. Before Jesus even mentioned her marital situation He offered her this hope. "Whoever drinks of this water will thirst again," He said, "but whoever drinks of the water that I shall give him will never thirst" (John 4:14).

Christ's goal was not to *get* a drink, it was to *give* one—from the fountain of living water that would change this woman from the inside out and radically change her future.

He was going somewhere with her. She was a part of His plan to reach this town with the Gospel. Although she didn't know it at the time, the moment Jesus revealed Himself to her as the Messiah, she was changed forever.

She placed her faith in Him. She now had a testimony of how Jesus revealed Himself to her and gave her living water so her soul would thirst no more.

## A CHANGED PERSON

But here's where the story gets even more interesting. What would she do as a result of her newfound salvation?

Would she go out and rebuke the town for ostracizing her because of her relational woes? This would have made her a bully.

Would she wallow around in guilt for how bad a sinner she was and refuse to tell anyone about what happened? This would have made her a bystander.

Although the Bible doesn't give us details on her salvation experience, it does tell us exactly what she did after her time with Jesus—"Many of the Samaritans from that town believed in Him because of the woman's testimony" (John 4:39).

She shared her testimony. Plain and simple. No frills. No polished sermon. No unique marketing plan to attract people to Jesus. She simply shared the story of how He changed her life.

And do you know what she became? A bridge between heaven and earth. She connected the heart of God with the hearts of those people, through the simple story of her testimony.

Jesus stood in the gap for her, and now it was her time to stand in the gap for others.

## POWER OF A TESTIMONY

The power of our testimony is the single greatest way to be that connection piece between God and others. A testimony is simply a God-story. It's the story of a time in your life when your faith intersected with God's faithfulness and it marked you forever. It starts with salvation but then continues as you grow in your faith.

A testimony is your story of how Jesus stood in the gap for you.

Sharing your testimony is how you stand in the gap for others.

## IT'S NOT BUSINESS, IT'S PERSONAL

Our business is one such testimony.

When we decided to franchise our real estate company back in 2007, we attended a conference that promised to teach us everything we needed to know about franchising a business. Well, that's at least what we went there for. Come to find out, it was a sales pitch for business owners to hire this group to franchise the companies for them.

I (Jason) remember sitting in a chair across from this sharp dressed, blonde-haired guy wearing a custom suit and shiny shoes. I felt out of place in my t-shirt and flip-flops. The more he talked, the more I was impressed. And the more I talked about our business and the niche we had, the more he was impressed. Needless to say, he wanted us to hire his company on the spot.

As I've learned in my business career, never make a decision when you feel pressure. Even though we didn't strike a deal that day I walked out of that meeting on cloud nine, knowing that not only was our idea good enough to be franchised, but I also found a company that could do all the hard work for us. Can't beat that!

The company promised they would handle all of the heavy lifting—paperwork, legal documents, structure, planning, budgets, marketing, sales, etc. The marketing and sales piece was the kicker for us—they promised to sell dozens of franchises within a one-year period, and we wouldn't have to lift a finger.

We thought God kicked a door wide open.

But cloud nine quickly turned into cloud one after we prayed about it. Although we had our hearts set on going the easy way with franchising by hiring this company to do it all for us, God prompted us to do it ourselves. Ouch.

He didn't stop there. Not only did He want us to build this thing from scratch, but God also impressed on us we were not supposed to market or advertise our franchise the conventional way. He spoke clearly to us about this, almost in an audible voice, telling us we were to sell our franchise locations by faith so when it grew only He could get the glory.

This new direction from God left us in a tough spot. We were not only supposed to turn this franchise-building company down, the one we really liked, but we were also *not* supposed to proactively try and sell franchises. Nice.

The more we thought about it, though, the more it began to make sense. The Bible was filled with stories of impossible situations where God came through in a big way. We knew He was asking us to do something like this so He could get all the credit.

What we didn't know then, but we know now, is God wanted to give us a testimony—a powerful story of a time where our faith intersected with His faithfulness that marked us forever and would become a tool we could use to help others in their journey.

After hearing this mandate from God, we honestly thought we might eventually have five franchisees at the most—and those would probably just be friends. So much for being men of faith, right?! The impossibility of what God asked us to do tested our faith.

Just so we're on the same page here—the conventional way to sell something is to figure out where the buyers are—this is marketing. Then you have to get your product or service in front of them—this is advertising. Finally, you have to convince them to buy—this is sales. That's Business 101. It was *this* process God told us *not* to do. You get the picture.

After a few days of whining to God, "Are you serious? We can't do this! How is anyone going to know about our franchise if we don't tell them?" we fully surrendered to doing it His way. Although we didn't know exactly what that looked like, we knew we were committed to obeying Him nonetheless.

When God leads, He may not tell you what's five steps ahead, but He'll always tell you what the next step is. And for us, that was to hire an attorney to handle the legal documents. At the same time, we worked frantically on our processes, procedures, manuals, and system. We literally manualized and systematized our entire business so anyone could do it (Jason: Even David).

Talk about a butt-kicker. That was a rough six months. When we were done, it felt like we ran a three-minute mile and coughed up a lung at the finish line. Never again. Ever.

With the legal work complete and a fully documented system in place, we had ourselves a full-blown franchise. But how was anyone going to know what we had to offer? This is where the fun began.

Instead of creating nifty ad slicks and engaging in a marketing campaign, which is what we typically would have done, we prayed. And prayed. And prayed.

A month later, we finally sold one to—drumroll please—a buddy in Texas. The second was—another drumroll please—a friend in Pennsylvania. Just like we thought—nothing but friends. We were thankful our friends knew what we were up to!

But three months later, with ZERO advertising, we got a call from someone we didn't know. He heard from someone who knew someone who was related to someone—that we had a unique franchise concept. After he came and heard our pitch, he signed on the spot.

Wow. We weren't expecting that. It felt really good.

The temptation to launch an ad campaign at that moment was overwhelming. Strike while the iron's hot, right? But we stuck to our conviction and did it the way God told us to.

A month later, our fourth franchisee signed up. Then a fifth. Then a sixth, and a seventh—until three years later, we had 100 franchisees in thirty-five states, all by word of mouth. We were featured that year in *Entrepreneur Magazine* as one of the fastest growing franchises in the nation. All without one penny sunk into a marketing and sales campaign.

Only God.

The success of that company put us on the map. We were featured in all sorts of magazines and newspapers, winning awards for innovation, sales production, speed of growth, and just about anything else you can think of. People from around the country were calling us wanting to know how we did it.

Our response was the same every time—"For us to take credit for building a successful company would be like a shovel taking credit for digging a hole. We're just the tools God chose to get the job done." We then let them in on our strategic marketing plan—"We get down on our knees and beg God to bring us just the right people."

A lot of folks didn't believe us. We understand. It is crazy. But there were a few who did, and they still talk with us today about how that story has impacted them.

This is the power of testimony.

It has nothing to do with us being uber-spiritual or super-bold. It has everything to do with simple obedience to the point where our faith intersected with God's faithfulness resulting in a testimony we can use forever—and a willingness to use it to bless others.

We have shared that testimony with countless entrepreneurs, not to talk them out of their marketing campaigns but to show them the power of trusting God more than their own ingenuity. The Lord knew we needed this lesson.

Two years later, in 2012, because of the success of our business, we got a call from a production company. "Hey, would you guys like to do a reality show? We think you'd be perfect for a network like HGTV."

And the rest, as they say, is history.

The book you're reading now is a result of that testimony.

You, too, have testimonies of God-moments where your faith intersected with His faithfulness a changed you forever. Tell them, as the Samaritan woman did in her city, and as we have done in our business. And don't let past failures keep you from being used by God—because your story can help others build their stories. When you do, you'll be a part of connecting people to Him. And soon you'll discover just how powerful your story truly is.

# CHAPTER 22

# LET'S GO FISHING

O nce you grasp the concept of how powerful a personal testimony is, you want to share it with the world. But the world's a pretty big place. We believe sharing your testimony is as simple as starting right where you are.

The CEO of our real estate company is an avid fisherman. He was also our roommate and teammate in college, so we've gotten to know him pretty well.

Tim Harrell grew up in Cape Town, South Africa, as a missionary kid. Most days he spent in the ocean trying to catch the perfect wave—the big kahuna he called it. He'd sit out on his surfboard for hours, catching a little wave here and there, just waiting for the big boy. And it didn't matter how cold the water was—he'd just slap on his wetsuit, and off he'd go. We asked him how he kept warm, and he told us he'd simply take a leak … in the suit. You've got to be pretty doggone cold to urinate on yourself for warmth.

Tim told us some pretty crazy missionary/surfer stories back when the three of us were cram-packed in that twelve- by twelve-foot dorm room at Liberty with nothing but two closets and a sink. I just remember how hungry we always were.

After college, we were all drafted into the pros, and Tim spent the next six years in the Dodgers organization. Then he moved his family to Charlotte to be with us, and we've been working together ever since. His surfing days in Cape Town have been replaced with a love for fishing—specifically salt-water fishing because he spent so much time in Vero Beach, Florida, with the Dodgers.

## FISHING FOR SHARKS

You should see him in action. In the same way he went after the big wave, he goes after the big shark. Not the massive great white, but a good-sized tiger shark that attracts a crowd on the beach and freaks everybody out as it flops around on the shore. It's fun to watch.

What's crazy about Tim, and I guess most avid fishermen, is the incredible preparation it takes to catch these sharks. It starts when he's at home prepping for our annual beach trip. He loads his three monster fishing poles, heavy-duty test wire, more lures and hooks than you can count, wire snips, tin snips, pliers, tackle boxes full of who knows what, white PVC pipes that go in the ground to hold the poles, a homemade carriage to carry everything, and a bright green kayak.

We typically arrive at the beach around 4:00 P.M., and after the cars are unloaded, Tim disappears. Within minutes we'll see him out with one of his poles and some of his gear, fishing like a normal human. He'll catch several fish, about eight to twelve inches in length, and plop them in a bait bucket. The next morning is when his fun begins.

He'll get up while it's still dark and go down to the water with all his gear. Fortunately, he's got an older son who loves to fish as well, so the two of them haul all the equipment while the rest of us snooze away.

His first item of business is to cut in half the fish he caught the previous day. Then he takes a massive hunk of bloody fish and puts it on this big hook attached to some heavy-duty line. At this point, it's typically daybreak, and our kids are hustling down to the beach for the much-anticipated kayak trip out into the deep with Uncle Tim.

When everything is ready, he hands the fishing pole to Mikey, his son, while he grabs the kayak and slides it into the water—all the while holding this bleeding hunk of fish that's now oozing down his arm. His other son, JJ, is usually the first to volunteer, because he sits in the back of the kayak, to hold the fish, so Tim can row out to the deep—way out to the deep.

If this freaks you out, we totally get it. The thought of letting one of your kids ride with a madman on a kayak in shark-infested waters while holding a bloody clump of fish is completely insane.

Forty-five minutes later, Tim and JJ arrive back on shore and the fishing begins. Usually, within an hour or so, a shark will bite and JJ will reel it in. Then the process starts all over again with another kid on the kayak until they've all had their turn on the water with good ole Uncle Tim.

We've caught some big ones in our day, and we've got an arsenal of good memories thanks to the time Tim takes to be the fisherman he is. The cool thing we've learned is fishing can teach us a lot about how to be a bridge for God.

## FISHING FOR PEOPLE

The disciple Peter was a fisherman long before Jesus recruited him. Jesus comes along and said, "I will make you a fisher of men." Interesting He didn't say, "I will *teach* you to fish for men." The promise was Jesus would transform Peter at the level of identity so he would want to fish for people more than he wanted to fish for fish. Now *that's* a miracle.

Fishing for fish is what prepared Peter to fish for people. As you've seen from our buddy, being a fisherman isn't an easy job. There's much that goes into it.

You can't just casually fish and expect to be good at it. And fish don't jump into your boat. You've got to take time, make the effort, and spend the money to be good at fishing. You've got to learn where to go, when to be there, and how to do it in a way that will catch the most fish. Of course, fishing for fish is both for food and fun, but fishing for people is for freedom from sin—the snares of Satan's power in someone's life. So, taking the time and making the preparations to fish for people is a rescue effort, not a sporting event.

Back in Bible times, fishermen didn't fish with a pole and lure like we do today. They typically went out when it was dark and shined a light over the side of the boat. The fish would be attracted to the light and swim toward the boat, having no clue a net was beneath them. Then the fisherman would pull the net and catch the fish.

## TIME TO FISH

When it comes to fishing for people, which isn't for sport but an act of generosity—a response to God's grace and kindness toward us, we must learn to fish with light, not lures. We don't put bait on a hook or rig up a shiny lure to attract people in an effort to "hook them" into our faith.

Rather, we shine our light in a dark world through good deeds and speaking the truth in love. And when people are attracted to the light, all we have to do is simply pull them in with the net of love. And when it comes to fishing for people, we have to apply the same discipline and diligence Tim does when fishing for fish. We must think proactively and make preparations to be the best we can be.

It all starts with a mindset. If you have accepted Christ as your Savior, you *are* a fisher of people. Your identity has already changed. Now you just have to act like it.

When your identity changes, it takes time for your brain to catch up with it so you start thinking like a changed person. It's like when we married our wives—we were no longer single, but it took a few years for us to stop thinking like bachelors. We couldn't just invite all the guys over anymore without first asking. (Jason: David messed that up a few times!)

Step two is to define where you will fish. These are the places where you do life—your work, your school, where you workout, the places you shop for groceries, your favorite local restaurants, etc.

Any place you frequently go is your spot, your "fishing hole" where you are to shine God's light. And when His light in you draws people, you simply introduce them to the Savior. Leading someone to the Lord, connecting them to their Creator for the very first time, is an exhilarating moment—way better than catching a fish.

One of our favorite "fishing holes" is our local CrossFit gym. We hate the workouts but love the people, like family. There's just something unifying about suffering with another human being. There's a sign above the door as you exit: "I hate you. I hate this place. See you tomorrow." That just about sums up what our workout community is like.

We don't go to the gym with our fishing poles and flashy lures to try to hook people into our *religion*. That's what cults do. We simply shine our light as best we can, always looking for an open door to share the reason for the hope we have. That's the key—you always have to be looking. To be a bridge for others, you must recognize everyone has a spiritual gap God wants to fill. The Holy Spirit will give you the opportunity to stand in the gap—you just have to be ready when it comes. Like one day after a workout, a guy came over to us all sweaty and said, "I think it's time we had the *God talk*. I've got some stuff I need to get off my chest."

If only it were always that easy every time. But we were ready, and he accepted Jesus. Now he's being discipled. It's all about being faithful at your "fishing hole."

## FINDING YOUR FISHING SPOT

We have another friend who happens to be the best fisher of men we've ever met. Everywhere he goes, he's got a fishing hole. You know some guys, like our buddy Tim, are just amazing fishermen and have no problem catching fish wherever they are? And they always have a few special places they consider "their spots." Well, our buddy, Scott Heldreth is the Tim Harrell of fishing for people.

We met him in 1994 at a pro-life outreach in Dallas. He was a preacher's kid gone wild, but by the time we met him, he had his life right with the Lord and was on fire for God.

You've heard the verse, "He who's been forgiven much loves much"? That's Scott's story. His was an absolute hellion, and when you listen to his testimony, you have to fight the tendency to think, "Dear Lord, please don't let that ever be my kid!"

But now he's a family man with eight kids and a passion for God that's contagious. While we wrote this book, he moved his family from Indiana to be here in Charlotte with us. Since he remodels homes for a living, one of his first items of business was to find a local supplier where he could get all his materials.

Back in Indiana, many of the employees at the hardware store where he shopped were sad about his moving away. The store manager asked for a meeting with him to see if there was any way he could stay. They loved his business, of course, but loved *him* most.

When he moved to Charlotte, one of the first things he said to us was, "Man, I need to figure out where I'm going to fish."

"Can't help you there," we said. "Ask Tim."

"No, I'm talking about making disciples. Loving people to Jesus."

A few days later, he came to us and said he visited three hardware stores before finding the one where he felt God wanted him to fish. We asked him, "What made you choose that one over the others?"

"I don't really know," he said. "I just asked the Holy Spirit to give me a gut feeling about it, and I didn't feel that until the third place. So, this is where I'm going to buy all my materials and start ministering to the people who work there."

Come on, Heldreth! You've got to give us more than that. We want a nice little three-step system that guarantees we'll hear God's voice and know exactly what to do. But that's not how it works. We're learning we have to be available for God, keep that light shining, and frequent the fishing hole often waiting for the Lord to draw them in.

To be a bridge that connects heaven to earth today, it's vital we understand the call to fish for people and the importance of establishing our "fishing holes" and keeping our light on while waiting for the catch!

# CHAPTER 23

# A SERVANT'S HEART

We love our mom. She took such good care of us as kids that, when we planted ourselves in North Carolina after professional baseball, we moved her and dad from Texas to be here with us. She helped us experience a little bit of heaven back then. But today she's experiencing all of heaven. She went home be with Jesus a few months before we started writing this book.

As painful as it is to think about life without her, the memory of how she lived burns in our hearts to this day. Reflecting on her life, we see how she modeled a life of service. She was always doing things for others. Come to think of it, we can't remember a time when Mom talked about herself. Her life was completely given for others, especially her family.

Mom had this amazing, incredible, low-drama/low-maintenance personality. That's one of the reasons everyone found her so easy to love. If you had a problem, she had ears to hear all about it. If you were hurt, she had the heart to help you through it. If you were hungry, she had an easy way to fix it. Whatever you needed she was there—always there.

We miss that about her. We miss the way she would respond when one of us would call and ask if we could drop the kids off while we took our wives out to eat. "Well of course," she would say. "I wanna see my babies."

By the time we got there, she would either have something whipped up for them to eat or she'd walk them to her pantry and let them choose away. All the grandkids loved Nana's pantry. "She's got the good granola bars! Ours taste like cardboard," they'd say. So much for trying to eat healthily. Thanks, Mom!

We especially miss the way she made us eggs, bacon, and cheese grits on a moment's notice. When we first started our business, our office was less than a mile from her house. By then, she didn't have the energy to walk a big cardboard box up to the office, but she was always thrilled when we stopped in for lunch, which was about three times a week. Stop judging us—you'd do it too!

We'd call with a quick heads up that we were on the way, and by the time we pulled into the driveway, we could smell the bacon. We'd barge through the front door, and she'd hand us plates as we barreled toward the stove for heaping portions of eggs and grits, enough to sink a ship.

No matter how hard we've tried to recreate this meal in our own homes, nothing we do tastes as good as what she made for us. Maybe it had something to do with the spoonful of bacon grease she scooped out of the Folgers Coffee can and slapped in the frying pan before she made the eggs. She taught us bacon grease is often the answer to many of life's problems.

The minute we finished eating, we were all hugs and kisses for the woman we loved so much.

## HOMEMADE T-SHIRTS

Mom found her joy in her grandkids too. Oh, did she ever love them. We joked that when the grandkids came along she forgot about us kids. She wasn't scared to let us know it either, especially when she wore T-shirts with their faces on them—every single day. Seriously, it's hard to recall a time she wasn't wearing a T-shirt with one of the grandkid's faces on it.

All grandparents have just a little something that makes them unique, and for our mom, it was these picture T-shirts. We have no clue where she had them all made. They popped up everywhere, sometimes with pictures we'd never seen before. She had a drawer full of them, all stamped with our kids' faces on the front. As we went through her belongings after she died, we found those shirts. One by one, we held them to our face and smelled the familiar scent of Nana. We each took one home, vowing to never wash it, to remember the woman we all loved so much.

Our mom died of lung disease that came on fast. From the day she was diagnosed to the time she passed, it was less than two weeks. Because her lungs took in such little air, it elevated her heart rate, so she was hooked up to the most powerful oxygen machine that existed. Yet, it still wasn't enough to keep her heart rate below 130 beats per minute. To put that in perspective, it was like she was running on a treadmill while trying to breathe through a straw, for a solid week! It was painful to watch.

## MORPHINE

Here's the most amazing part of the story. The doctors explained that, when patients receive a terminal diagnosis such as Mom's, they typically prescribe morphine to keep the patients comfortable in death. The only problem, however, was that it might also put her to sleep for the last time. The idea, according to the doctors, would be that Mom could drift into death without feeling any pain.

To be honest, we all hated seeing her struggle to breathe, so we asked her to consider it. But she would have nothing to do with it. She couldn't even talk—all she did was shake her head "No" as violently as she could. The doctors were dumbfounded. They didn't understand why someone who was going through so much pain would refuse the very medication that could take it away from her.

But that's the beauty of our mother—she didn't want anything to take away her ability to be fully present with her family, even if she had to sacrifice her own comfort. Before she was admitted into the intensive care unit, she refused morphine and told the doctors she wanted to be fully awake and aware with her family. And when it got really tough, instead of giving in she bared down.

Before things got worse everything seemed fine, even with her elevated heart rate. They initially gave her steroids, and for a few days, they helped immensely. So much so we couldn't get her to stop talking. She talked nonstop for three days. It was a blast! She had so much fun enjoying her friends and family.

One time, she even looked over at my (Jason's) in-laws, who stopped in for a visit, and said with great enthusiasm, "I don't know a lot about these steroids, but I LIKE 'EM!"

Soon we discovered the disease was still spreading in her lungs despite the strength of the steroids. That's when we knew the end was soon.

We all took turns being with her in the hospital during the final few days. And just before she passed, we were all jam-packed into the room just looking at her as she lay there, barely able to open her eyes. Her gasps were short and quick as she would arch her back to breathe. Our hearts broke for her, knowing all her pain could end if she would simply take the morphine.

But every now and then, she'd open her eyes, just for a few seconds, and look around. Dad said, "She's taking it all in. She knows we're here."

We all stood there, fighting back tears so Mom wouldn't worry about us. This amazing woman who sacrificed so much for us was making this one final sacrifice to simply be present with us—it was gut-wrenching. One by one, we walked over and kissed her head, taking it in because we knew she might not make it through the night. Nobody said a word. We just stood there in somber silence as worship music played lightly in the background.

For the next few days, we watched as she hung on with every ounce of strength she had. Every now and then, she'd moan. It took us a while, but we quickly discovered she was saying, "Coke." If the last wishes of a dying woman were for a Coke, then Coke is what she got!

Those were difficult days to watch. There were times when her oxygen levels would dip so low her lips turned blue. The machine buzzer would go off, and the nurses would come in to try to get her back to normal. Each time that happened, the palliative doctor (the one who's supposed to help you die well) would come in and offer mom morphine. "NO!" she would cry out, barely able to voice the word.

By this point, all of us kids agreed, telling her, "Mom, it's okay to take morphine. We'll be here with you." But the issue for Mom wasn't that we would be with her—she wanted to be with us. She wanted to stay conscious, so she could be fully present. Having been a nurse, she'd seen how morphine removes a person's ability to fight. And fight is what she did, right up to the very end. Man, did she ever fight.

Those last few days changed our lives forever. We saw our mom endure such immense pain so she could be with us, hold our hands, hear our voices, listen to worship music with us, and catch a glimpse of each grandkid when she could muster the strength to open her eyes.

## LOVE SPEAKS

On the last night of her life I (Jason) and my daughter Allie slept in the hospital room with her. David was there too. We made a pallet on the floor behind her bed. Allie was such a trooper. She stayed up all night long to be with her, helping adjust her mask or get her a drink, whatever she could do to make Nana comfortable. At this point, Mom hadn't said much for three days.

At about 1:00 A.M., while lying on the cold hard floor and listening to all the beeping noises from the machines, I woke up and saw Allie leaning over Mom's bed. She was just staring at her Nana while holding her hand. Mom's oxygen levels had dipped so low I thought it was only a matter of hours before we would lose her. But at that moment, right when I thought mom was unconscious, I heard her gently whisper in the faintest voice, "I … love … you … Allie." She could barely get the words out, but I heard it. David heard it too. Even more importantly, Allie heard it.

Mom died that afternoon. But not before she gave her granddaughter an experience that will mark her life forever, something she will cherish until the day she goes to be with Nana in Heaven.

In her final moments before she passed away, Mom grabbed our dad's hand and looked at him with tired eyes. We knew this was the end.

Then she looked above him and in an instant of what looked like pure exhilaration she looked up, opening her eyes as wide as she could get them. She had a look of wonder and amazement in her eyes, like "Oh wow!" Then she breathed her last.

We're not sure what she saw with her last breath, but she saw something—and it was good. It serves as a small exclamation point on a life well lived.

## THE POWER OF SACRIFICE

Looking back at her life and then seeing her in those final days, painstakingly present with all of us, we clearly saw her servant-heart was fueled by her sacrificial-heart. It reminded us how Jesus was offered wine to dull the pain as He was on the cross, yet He refused. He wanted to be fully present to carry out every detail of God's plan. And what a sacrifice it was!

Our mom modeled a sacrificial life. In her final moments on earth, she gave each one of us a small touch from heaven. She could have easily taken the morphine and simply died in her sleep. But she didn't. She sacrificed that for something greater, for the chance to be there with all of us. Now we will forever have the memory of those last days with her. Allie will forever have the memory of that "I love you" from her Nana— all because of our mom's willingness to sacrifice.

Mom was never on stage or prominently featured in any setting at any time during her life, but she was a powerful example of how a life of sacrifice brings heaven to earth for those you love. She may have seemed small and insignificant in the world's eyes, but to our family, she was strong and indispensable.

We have no idea if our mom's ability to sacrifice by putting others first was something she worked hard at or if it was just a quality she was born with. All we know is her sacrificial life helped bridge heaven and earth for our family and for hundreds of those who knew and loved her. And we want to be that too, both in her memory and for the sake of Christ.

## CHAPTER 24

# RED LIGHT/GREEN LIGHT

Although God calls us to stand in the "personal" gap for others, creating that divine connection, there are times when God wants us to also stand in the "cultural" gap for truth.

In Nehemiah's time, God's people were called to build and battle. They held a trowel in one hand to build the city and a sword in the other hand to battle God's enemies. Of course, people are not our enemies, as Paul taught the Ephesians, but rather we fight the spiritual forces of darkness that seek to redefine truth, remove God, and reshape culture.

## TRAFFIC LIGHTS

We made it to the stage and took our seats as several thousand people stood on the lawn waiting for the program to begin. Protestors gathered at nearly every corner, screaming, "Don't force your beliefs on me," as news cameras swirled all over the place. We were in Raleigh, North Carolina, just outside the capital building with several public officials and other invited guests to voice our support for a recently passed bill reinforcing restroom and locker room use to biological sex—men in men's bathrooms and women in women's bathrooms.

The view held by those shouting at us was a person's gender can change based on how they feel at the time. This would mean a forty-year-old male who felt like a sixteen-year-old female should be able to use the women's restroom.

By the time we were announced to speak, the crowd was pretty worked up. All I (David) remember is the minute Jason grabbed the microphone he said, "On the count of three, I want you all to say the word 'MOP' five times really fast."

The crowd looked at him confused. The lawmakers on the stage had no clue where he was going. But they were willing to comply.

"One—Two—Three," he said.

"MOP, MOP, MOP, MOP, MOP," the crowd shouted.

"What do you do at a green light?" he asked.

"STOP!" they replied, only to erupt in laughter a few seconds later when they realized what they said.

"You can stop at a green light if you want," he said with a smile. "But I think I'll just go!"

Jason's always been riskier than I am when we speak. But I could tell his little humor tactic worked because the crowd looked anxious for an explanation.

"Your brains just told you something that didn't line up with reality," he explained. "Can you imagine what would happen to traffic if just 5 percent of the drivers in this city decided green meant stop and red meant go? You wouldn't be able to get anywhere on the roads."

By the time I got up there, I chimed in, "Our culture is treating biology the same way. God is the One Who created us—that's reality. If we refuse to operate by that reality, it will be like stopping on green and going on red—chaos will be the result. Civil society cannot function without laws based on objective truth."

## WHAT'S YOUR STANDARD?

Our reasoning made sense to the crowd. They recognized the minute we allow people to define what's right and wrong for themselves everything breaks down from there. This is why the Founders of America established our nation "under God," because they properly recognized you cannot build anything apart from an objective, immovable, unchangeable standard of truth.

Good laws are based on an *objective* standard for people's safety, not a *subjective* standard for people's comfort. That's a crucial point to know in these hot-button, cultural conversations.

But we live in a time when "under God" has been exchanged for "without God" because people seek to define their own truth. The idea of an objective standard of right and wrong is not politically correct anymore. Even worse, if people dare to make a truth claim, especially if it comes from the Bible, they're often smeared as haters, bigots, and intolerant.

If you would've told us two years earlier we'd be called haters for saying a man should use the men's restroom, we would have told you it was more likely for the Dallas Cowboys to change their colors to green and gold and replace the star on their helmets with a big G. Not a chance!

Although we don't doubt some people have mixed feelings about their gender, redefining an entire system of reality isn't the answer. And although we love those who struggle with these issues, we also cannot sit silently as society disconnects from reality. Changing the traffic lights because a few people aren't comfortable with the color scheme would be disastrous.

In response to this North Carolina law protecting bathrooms, political leaders from other states threatened North Carolina with boycotts and travel bans. Professional athletes and Hollywood stars started weighing in. The NCAA even pulled a sex-segregated sporting event out of our state because we have sex-segregated bathrooms. The hypocrisy was mind-numbing. By the time Bruce Springsteen canceled his concert in North Carolina, we could see the cultural gap widening to a point where we had to take a stand. That's when we got the invitation to speak in Raleigh.

But we were afraid. We didn't want to endure the same brutality of insults that flew our way when we were fired by HGTV. And we were afraid because we had no clue what to say.

Then, as I (David) was up one morning early pacing in my living room, I prayed about what God had to say about all this. That's when I heard a gentle whisper in my spirit, "Traffic lights."

What? The house was dead quiet. I waited.

"Traffic lights." I heard again.

I had no clue what the Lord was saying to me.

I started meditating on it. I closed my eyes and began thinking about all the cars whisking in and out of traffic on any given day, stopping at lights, waiting for other cars to pass, and then proceeding again. I saw various colors, shapes, and sizes of cars. And I saw all the different people driving them. They were also various colors, shapes, and sizes too, but they also had different beliefs, backgrounds, and views about life. In my mind, I saw incredible diversity, which was the buzzword being promoted in the news so loudly at the time.

Then it began to make sense. God loves diversity. Heck, He created it! But He also gave us order—laws to govern our actions so we can live together and flourish in society as a diverse people. Traffic works not because everybody agrees on everything—quite the contrary. Traffic works because, despite the incredible diversity of beliefs and backgrounds among the drivers, they all agree on one thing: Red means stop and green means go. There is an objective truth to which everyone submits. The result is we can drive to work or the store or the ballgame—wherever we want—in safety.

As I envisioned the reality of drivers ignoring the objective standard, "red means stop, and green means go," I could easily see how chaos would erupt in the streets. If all people did what was right in their own eyes, stopping and going whenever they wanted, the once-free flow of traffic would quickly end. The result would no longer be safety but danger. This is tragically illustrated when someone runs a red light and crashes into someone going on green.

So, when Jason stood on stage and made the traffic light joke, he actually stole the analogy God gave me. But we have used it over and over again when talking about the widening gap in our culture.

Because today, America has become eerily similar to the time of the judges in the Old Testament when "everyone did what was right in their own eyes."

## CHAOS OR CALM

Check out what Judges 5:6–8 says, in light of our traffic analogy, "In the days of Shamgar son of Anath, and in the days of Jael, people avoided the main roads, and travelers stayed on winding pathways. There were few people left in the villages of Israel—until Deborah arose as a mother for Israel. When Israel chose new gods, war erupted at the city gates."

A distinct gap in culture existed during this time in Israel's history—a chaotic disconnect between heaven and earth—causing people to literally "avoid the main roads." The result was *war at the city gates.* The Hebrew word used for "war" here literally means "chaos." This happened when people refused to honor the truth of God because they rejected the God of truth, and chaos was the result.

But the most important part of that passage isn't how chaos erupted—it's about how God chose to calm it. He sent a woman named Deborah to stand in the gap as a mother in Israel, to bring clarity where there was confusion by standing for truth in a culture of lies. She led her nation back to being "under God" and refused to let it remain "without God."

## DO LIKE DEBORAH

Our primary role as believers is to stand in the *personal gap* by loving people as we reveal to them the truth that sets us free. You've read many of these stories in this book. But we also have the responsibility to stand in the *cultural gap* by connecting God's truth to a disconnected culture. God calls faithful people to stand in this gap like Deborah in her generation.

Although it looks different for each of us and certainly we don't have to take the stage in our state's capital, we can each still lovingly enter the conversation. When God's truth is being trampled and people are suffering, we must.

If we don't, who will?

Unfortunately, many Christians have "abandoned the roads" for fear of offending someone or being called something they are not. But God is calling believers back, to stand in the gap and reconnect His truth to a disconnected world. He's calling us to live out His prayer "thy Kingdom come, thy will be done on EARTH as it is in HEAVEN" for our nation. God raised Deborah in her generation, as well as Nehemiah in his—both were provoked to take action and did so boldly. And yet both were motivated by love—a love for God that compelled them to stand in the gap whatever the cost.

# CHAPTER 25

# DON'T TAKE THE GIRL

**W**hen she stepped out of the car that bright sunny day in Bluefield, West Virginia, I (Jason) could feel my knees go weak. The summer breeze blew her hair like she was walking down a runway in a movie. For one brief moment, I didn't know my name, where I was, or why I was even there. I only knew one thing—I felt alive, more alive than ever before.

She was wearing cute khaki shorts and a royal blue tank top. I was captured by her smile—and everything else. I knew right then and there I wanted to marry her. I had never been so sure of anything in my life.

This isn't a "love at first sight" story. I had known Tori for just more than a year and grew close with her family. As we mentioned back in chapter one, David and I spent a summer in her hometown of Torrington playing baseball for the newly founded Torrington Twisters. Torrington defined New England small-town charm. Chock-full of people with Italian and Polish roots, we quickly learned "Hello" was not an acceptable greeting—it was "How ya doin?"

## ITALIAN LESSONS

It didn't take long for us to learn the code—when people said, "How ya doin?" the proper response was "How YOU doin?" with a little emphasis on the "you," just so they knew you cared.

Tori's dad, Fert, spoke thicker Italian than any man we'd met. And when I say Fert was Italian, I mean *Italian*. Everything about him screamed "I'm Italian, whatchoo gonna do about it? Oh, and while you're staring at me, go get me a *hawt dawg*!"

He was a principal at a local Christian school and the associate pastor of the church. The first Sunday we were in town, he invited all the guys to come to service the following week. David and I were the only two who showed up.

After the service, Fert took us back into his office to chat. While we were in there, I saw on the wall a framed pencil drawing of a woman. She was stunningly beautiful.

"Who's that?" I asked. "That's my daughter," he responded. I felt my heart leap out of my chest. He added, "If you guys come to the graduation ceremony we're having tomorrow night, I'll introduce you to her and the rest of my family."

"Uh, that won't be a problem at all," I thought. At this point in my life, I had only one more year of college and no prospects for a Mrs. Benham on the horizon. Meeting a new girl was a welcome idea. David and Lori were already a thing (when she realized our freshman year she couldn't have me, she had to settle for second best).

The next night, we showed up. After the service was over, a girl in a lime green dress walked right up to us with a joyful confidence I wasn't used to. She offered her hand and said, "Hi! I'm Tori."

"I'm Jason. And this is my twin sister David," I responded.

"I'm Frank's daughter," she said. And with those words, my heart sank. Not because it wasn't nice meeting the girl I saw in the picture, but because she was younger than I expected. She was six years younger than me. I was about to be a senior in college and she wasn't even done with high school yet. Ugh! That was a problem.

## IF ONLY

Thoughts of *if only she were older* crossed my mind a thousand times that summer. But she wasn't, and that was that.

I knew she'd make a great wife for some lucky guy one day. My brother and I even tried setting her up with one of our younger buddies.

"You gotta meet this girl," I said to him. "She's gonna make the best wife and is going to be a knock-out one day."

I think they went on a date or something. I think. I don't remember, and I don't want to ask Tori. I'm starting to get that hot feeling in my chest as I even think about the idea of her going on a date with another guy.

I need to stop writing now …

Ok, I'm back. I had to get up and walk around to get my game face back on.

Little did I know a year later, a knock-out punch was headed my way. The year after I played in Torrington, I was drafted by the Baltimore Orioles and sent to their rookie team in Bluefield, West Virginia, to play. Halfway through the season, Fert brought his family for a visit.

That's when I saw her again—right there in the parking lot of the hotel—no longer the same young girl I once knew—a full-blown woman. Tori Cantadore. It's amazing what can happen in a years' time.

But I wasn't the only guy who noticed her that day. I was with a teammate of mine who immediately leaned over and asked, "Who the heck is that?"

"She's too young for you, dude," I responded, knowing I needed to call off the dogs before the chase began.

I played the protective brother card, but in my heart, I was feeling much more than just a brother. I wanted to become her hero. I had never felt for someone what I felt at that moment. It was a little scary for me— like going out in uncharted water in a kayak.

## GAME TIME

That night, she and her real brother, Frankie (who I nicknamed "Dinga"—but that's another story), stayed with the host family where my teammate buddy and I lived. They had an extra room, so they invited them to stay. And yes, this was the same buddy from the parking lot.

The four of us stayed up late, talking and laughing into the night. At one point, I went upstairs to call my parents and tell them about the game. Mom and Dad waited up every night to hear how David and I played. (He was in Lowell playing for the Red Sox rookie team). That night, I had more to talk about than just baseball—I told them what I was feeling for Tori. They met her the summer before when they came to Torrington for a visit. Instantly they both said, "We knew the minute we met her she was someone special. We hoped maybe you'd be willing to wait for her."

That's all I needed to hear.

When I came back downstairs, Frankie had nodded off. While he was drooling on the couch pillow, I looked over and there was my buddy, sitting closer to Tori than he was before, lost in conversation. I could tell by the way he was talking with her he wasn't interested in just getting to know her—he was interested in pursuing her.

I felt a hot anger well up in my chest. Not like an "I'm going to punch you in the face" kind of anger, but more like a "back off before I remove your arms and legs" kind. Ha! Not really, but it's fun to think that way. He was a good guy with no ill intentions, at least I think.

What I truly felt was a protectiveness that came over me, like something of mine was being threatened. She wasn't really mine, but it felt like she was. My buddy knew what a catch she was, and it sure looked like he was moving in for the kill.

This was uncharted emotional territory for me. I had never felt protective over a girl like this before.

The fact was, I loved her. I really loved her, I just didn't realize it until then. I grew to love her as a friend, and then this new romantic spark sealed the deal in my heart.

I marched across the living room and sat right between them. I didn't care a lick what my buddy or even Tori thought about it. I plopped down between them, changed the conversation, and sat there in a "not over my dead body" pose for the rest of the evening.

Tori ended up going upstairs to bed, while I and—uhemm, the unmentionable—slept in the living room listening to Dinga snore all night.

## VIGILANCE FOR LOVE

It was this feeling of jealousy that stuck out to me most. As I lay awake that night I stared at the ceiling pondering the thought of Tori and me living our lives together. The more I thought about her, the more that feeling came over me. *I don't want another dude to grab her up and take her away from me*, I thought.

It was a good kind of jealousy that seeks to protect—like what God feels for us. For me, this was the final piece to the puzzle in my heart. I knew if I felt this way for her, I had to pursue her. I hadn't felt like that for any other girl before.

Being the activator I am, the day her family was leaving Bluefield I pulled Fert aside, "Hey, uh, Fert. Can we talk?"

"Howya doin, bud?" he replied. "You wanna hawt dawg?" Not really. He just said, "What's up?"

"I think I'm having feelings for your daughter," I choked out, waiting anxiously for the response I hoped he'd give.

"Yeah, we know," he said. "Last summer Kristen and I both knew you were the one for her. We just didn't know when you guys would realize it."

That's all I needed to hear.

Not long after, we started dating and two years after that the wedding bells rang in Torrington! It's been eighteen years as of writing this book, and we are more madly in love today than ever before.

I will never forget that night in Bluefield when protective jealousy flooded my soul like the breaking of a dam. To be honest, there have been a few other times in our relationship where I've felt the same feeling, but nothing like that first night. I've come to realize if you're truly in love with your spouse, it will happen from time to time—and it's a good thing.

We should have a jealous love for our spouse—the Godly kind that's protective, not the evil kind that's envious. Godly jealousy protects that which is mine. If we don't have a good dose of healthy jealousy in our relationship, it proves our love may not be as deep as we thought it was. It's the type of jealous love God has for us: "for the Lord, whose name is Jealous, is a jealous God" (Exodus 34:15).

## CARING DEEPLY FOR WHAT'S RIGHT

Those who stand in the gap for others operate out of a spirit of love—a deep love for God and the people He created. Typically, we think this means we're supposed to feel all "ooey-gooey-mushy" about the Lord, where we want to sit on His lap while He holds our head against His chest. But that's only one aspect of love. What I discovered that night in Bluefield is the love also feels like a holy fire burning inside your chest as it seeks the protection and affection of the one you desire.

How often do we feel that for God? He certainly feels that for us. What goes on in our hearts when His reputation is smeared in culture, when He is misrepresented, when He is mocked and even cursed? Do we feel a holy jealousy to protect the One we desire—to sit between Him and the gross mischaracterization of Him? How about when His kids are being persecuted for living out their faith? Are we jealous enough to stand in the gap for them too because we love God's family?

If I overheard someone bad-mouthing Tori or saying false things about her but I just blew it off and acted like it was no big deal, what would that communicate about my love? Or what if I sat there and said nothing in her defense because I feared what people would think of me? What kind of love is that?

It would not be love. Because love looks like something, and sometimes it looks like a good dose of righteous jealousy—one that protects and defends. Throughout the Bible, we see the jealous love of God for us because we are the apple of His eye and the jewel of His creation. He doesn't want the devil to snatch us away from Him. He wants our affection, and He offers us His protection. But how jealous are we for Him? If we love Him, we should be. If we're going to stand in the gap, we have to be.

## JEALOUS FOR TRUTH

I (Jason) saw this concept of holy jealousy for God lived out by Tori once when we were on vacation. It surprised me because she's probably the least confrontational person I've ever known. Engaging in conflict for her runs a close second to the thought of smooching me in the morning before I brush my teeth—it ain't happening.

I'll let her tell the story.

We'd just arrived for our annual beach trip with my side of the family. We unpacked the car at the condo. The smell of my mom's cooking officially welcomed us to vacation, so I plopped down on the freshly made bed to scroll through Facebook. Vacation seems to welcome these types of indulgences.

"Christian artist comes out gay" blasted across my news feed several times. That was an attention grabber, for sure, but I was quickly distracted by my kids' sunscreen-plastered faces, begging me to hit the beach. So, I dropped the phone on the bed and headed out to the salty air.

After dinner, a walk on the beach, baths, and kisses goodnight, I dropped back onto the bed where my phone was waiting. This time, I saw a message from a friend right away.

"Have you seen all the articles circulating about the Christian singer leaving his wife and kids?" she asked. "He professes Jesus as Lord yet is leaving his family because he's attracted to men—and he's being hailed a hero for doing it. Our cousin is struggling with the same thing and articles like these make it tough because we love him so much, want him to embrace the freedom He has in Christ, and live in the power of that freedom. We need help."

After an hour or so of reading various articles along with the comment threads beneath, my brain hurt almost as much as my heart. It was mass confusion. The thought of my kids soon having to navigate truth through the tornado of stories and opinions such s this on social media had me wide awake. I rested my head on the headboard, staring at a starfish hanging on the wall. Then I remembered a comment from one of my favorite pastors. It echoed through my brain, "What does love require of you?"

So, I turned back to my phone. What were the Christian leaders saying on social media—the ones I respected and trusted? What did their love for God require of them at this moment as leaders of people in a culture embracing a lie? In the whirlwind of confusion, I was craving truth communicated with compassion and clarity. But I couldn't find anything. Nobody was speaking up about this very public media story.

"It will take time," I told myself.

## STILL NOT RESOLVED

Vacation was coming to an end, and although our days were filled with play and togetherness by the sea, below the surface I felt the tension of that lingering question in my head, "What does love require of you?" I'd begun to see the phrase, "Love wins" repeatedly over the last few months in articles imploring me to let people love whomever they want. But, what did they mean by love?

I didn't want to keep reading, and I definitely didn't want to say anything on social media. I was on vacation, after all. I'd rather ignore it all and enjoy life. That would be the easiest approach. Avoid conflict, keep the peace, and make everyone happy. That's my natural bent anyway.

But I am a parent of four kids. If I took this same approach of keeping quiet about truth to avoid conflict with my kids, I wouldn't be loving them well at all. I can't take the easy way out and avoid tough conversations. Well, the truth is I can and sometimes do. But it doesn't end well in the long term for them; that's for sure.

"What does love require me to do?"

The more I thought about it, the more I realized love doesn't win, love has already WON! And because love won—at the cross through the death of Jesus—we can live powerfully in that love through a transformed life in Him. We aren't the same anymore. We don't find our identity in our sinfulness or sexuality—we find our identity in Christ as we walk in victory. "That's the win people are really searching for," I thought.

"We really need help with this," I began to pray. "Lord, raise up a well-respected pastor who will bring clarity to this issue for your people.

The words "What does love require of you?" again fell back on me.

## WHO WILL STAND IN THE GAP?

I felt strongly I needed to call the pastor who preached the sermon where I learned to ask this question. He also happens to be one of the best communicators of biblical truth I've ever heard. I didn't know how to communicate what I was feeling inside, so I guess you could say I was calling in the big dogs for help. I thought about how much it would help my friend with her cousin if this pastor would bring some clarity to the confusion over sexual identity.

I called his church and left a message. Within a day, a representative from the leadership team called me back. I explained the reason for my call and asked if the pastor ever made a public statement about marriage and sexual identity and if he hasn't would he consider doing it now in light of the firestorm of opinions circulating among Christians over this particular issue.

I don't do stuff like this—ever. But, I felt a fire deep in my heart that would not allow me to sit silently as the truth of God's design for sexuality was twisted in a whirlwind of public opinion.

I told her, in a time when sexual identity is being defined by sexual liberty, it seems love requires us to communicate the truth of God that can set people free as they find their true identity in Christ.

"But the problem is," I said, "it seems the church is divided on this topic. So, I guess my question is—as your pastor once taught my husband and me—what does love require of us today? We need help communicating truth with love and compassion. Your pastor has such a gift of

communicating the truths of God's word—how is he articulating this in
your church?"

"Our official response," she responded with hesitation in her voice,
"is that we are intentionally vague on this topic. We purposefully do not
address this at our church."

"If we got into this discussion," she continued, "half our congregation would leave."

Pause. I took a deep breath as I tried to process her response.

"But right now," I responded, knowing I needed to press in, "the
world is asking the question publicly. To avoid the truth we know sets
people free seems ..." I paused for a moment, "well, not very loving."

"That's your tension," she responded. "That's just your way of making yourself feel better." She then proceeded to tell me how we tend to
make issues like this more about ourselves than the person we are trying
to love—I was somehow operating out of guilt, and this wasn't good.

"I really don't think so," I responded. "If it were just about me,
I would let it go and get on with life. My nature is to be that person who
just understands and affirms the things that make everyone feel
happy. I really like to be liked. But protecting myself and my reputation
over someone's well-being and soul doesn't seem to be the proper posture
for Christians. It's not what love requires of me, right?"

The conversation went on for some time but progressed no further.
It was "my tension," she said several times. Her voice was kind and calm
as she made it very clear why this particular pastor was radio silent on
this important issue.

I reached out in the hope the pastor I so admired for all those years
would actually share the only truth that sets people free, instead of letting
people "guess" what that truth is. I felt a *jealousy* for the truth of God
rise inside of me. I couldn't just sit silent, even though everything in me
wanted to.

It made me think of Paul's words when he said, "You have many
teachers but few fathers" (1 Corinthians 4:15). This pastor is my favorite

teacher of all time. He's so good. But along with good teachers, we need mothers and fathers who will lovingly stand in the gap for others by applying God's truth in all areas of life, even when it could cost them something.

Everything in me wanted to stay out of it. But asking that simple question—"what does love require of me?"—wouldn't let me. I have since learned asking this question in other areas of my life helps me overcome the natural fears that have caused me to shrink back in the past.

I ended up talking with my friend about her cousin's struggles and encouraged her to lovingly point to the freedom Jesus brings. I refused to remain "intentionally vague" about it. How could I be, when I know the truth that sets people free?

Looking back, I now realize God used that phone call not to get this pastor to stand for truth, but to teach *me* to do it. The entire situation evoked jealousy in me to bring the love of Jesus wherever it is needed most. It may not always bring the results I am hoping for, like that phone call, but asking the simple question "what does love require of me?" keeps me accountable to move toward things from which I am inclined to run.

I have learned love looks like something. It causes me to get outside myself, my natural bents and fears. It asks me to stand in the vacant spaces where only love can bridge the gap—the spaces where "Your kingdom come" moments are waiting for me.

And you know, every day looks different. When I start every day with that simple question, "what does love require of me?" it's a call to action every time. Today, for me that looked like spending the afternoon in a gymnasium practicing volleyball with two anxious fourteen-year-olds who are now at tryouts as I type. Tonight will look like celebrating a victory or nursing a wound and a "we'll get 'em next year babygirl." Either way, I'm committed to being the bridge that brings the love of Jesus today.

# CHAPTER 26

# LOVE IN ACTION

A sking the question, "What does love require of me?" is a call to action that starts at home—because Satan wants to destroy the family, and marriage is at the top of his list. So, if we find ourselves fighting *against* our spouse instead of *alongside* him/her we'll miss golden opportunities to stand in the vacant spaces where love in action can bridge the gap.

A few years ago, Sara Montague walked into church about a half hour into the service and quietly sat down on the front row. She didn't look up or greet anyone; she just sat there, clearly in pain. I (David) was preaching that day, and I could tell something was wrong. She had been with us before on Sundays in the past but always with her husband. This day, however, she was alone.

I felt I needed to say something, but I didn't know what to do. After services ended, one of the men from church went over to greet her. He asked her where her husband, Cory, was, and she broke down crying, saying he had left town and was done with the marriage. Within seconds, he gathered the women of the church together and ministry with her began.

Meanwhile, another man from the church went outside to call Cory. After being convinced to come home, he and Sara ended up reconciling within a few weeks. It's amazing enough to see what God did in their marriage, but even more amazing is how He then used them together, as a united force, to put love into action and stand in the gap for someone else. God worked *in* them and then worked *through* them, so we want you to hear their story.

## CORY

Soon after Sara and I were married, we began to struggle with our relationship. Many couples say that first year is the worst, but I would say this felt different. Deeper. Like everything around us was trying to tear us apart.

We came into this relationship with a lot of baggage and refused to leave it at the curbside before we entered our new lives together.

We had started going to church with David and Jason, making new friends, worshipping God, trying to put on our newlywed faces and act like we had it all together. Yet, this struggle, this tug of war between make-it-work and give-it-up was tearing us up.

We didn't talk about it. Just suffered separately, alone. Sometimes the dam burst, and we'd get into these huge arguments. Big things at first triggered the fights, but then it was the little things. That's when we knew we were in deep trouble.

I didn't like the whole church scene because people were getting up into my business, where they might realize I was really a phony. So I started pulling away from the church, then from Sara. Six months into our marriage, I left town and moved to Florida to be with my family.

## SARA

Cory left me all alone in an empty house—I was devastated. I knew he had given up on me. It was crushing to feel that rejection so early in the marriage. I had been preparing for this moment my whole life, and now I was about to become a divorce statistic.

I unloaded everything on my mom, and she calmly, peacefully said, "Stand your ground." I was thinking, "Are you kidding? This guy's being a jerk to me. I can do better. I need to go." But she said, "Pray for him and don't stop praying for him. I'm not going to stop praying for you guys. Don't go anywhere. Now get back in that church!"

That was quite a moment for me. It made sense. I was operating on emotions, but she was speaking truth, spiritual truth, wisdom into my life. (Cory: I'm so glad she did!)

I did all the things Mom told me to do. I went to church the next Sunday, and one of the men ran up and said, "Hi Sara, where's Cory?" Great.

I fought all the emotions, trying to play it cool, so I said, "Oh, Cory moved out." That's when cool fell to the wayside and emotional wreck took over. I started bawling my eyes out. Soon the folks around me surround me and prayed the sweetest prayer.

## CORY

During that time, one of the guys from church reached out to me and asked all kinds of questions. He then took me out for coffee and listened as we talked about those dark, hidden places I'd kept secret for too long. Meanwhile, the ladies at church surrounded Sara with all kinds of love and support.

Then that same guy bought Sara and me each a Life Application Bible. I believe that's really why we are where we are today. The Word of God. The truth started to penetrate all the lies we'd been believing.

I had chased the things of this world, looking for contentment and satisfaction in temporary things that deteriorate and die away. It's the standard I brought into our marriage, expecting Sara to bring me contentment and satisfaction in my life. She could never live up to that standard.

Only Jesus could.

I came back to North Carolina, started going to church, listening to all those powerful sermons, digging into the Bible, and realizing how sinful I was. And the weight of my sin broke me down. I prayed,

>"Lord, in obedience and faith, I'm going to move back home.
> I want to start opening up your Word every single day. I'm
> going to dig into this. I have no strategy on how it's going to

work, but all I'm going to do is trust in you, Jesus. So I'm surrendering to You, and as I dig in your Word, whatever you have for me, I want."

Sara and I talked about it and decided I'd move back home. We resolved to make our marriage work. Only truth and a deep conviction could lead me back home and back to the marriage God intended for us to have.

## SARA

I wish I could say it was easy from that moment on, but it wasn't. It was very hard. I harbored resentment toward Cory, even in the way he read the Bible every day. I said to myself, "Does he think he's better than me for reading the Bible?" I'm not proud of it, but this was the stuff going through my head. It took some time until I realized God was actually changing Cory right before my eyes. It was incredible. It wasn't an act or a competition. It was the truth of God changing someone right before my eyes.

Maybe I didn't want to accept Cory's transformation because it meant I had to change too. I realized that I never understood what a relationship with Jesus was all about. I'd been lukewarm as a Christian. A church-goer but not a real Jesus-lover. As I started pouring into the Life Application Bible, I saw it. I got it. I could see Jesus throughout the whole Bible, pursuing people throughout history, wanting to connect them back to Himself. All of us, including me.

## CORY

God shaped Sara and me into new people for a new chapter in our lives. Not only did we want to make our marriage the best for God, but we also wanted to serve Him together as well. Instead of facing off in opposition, we decided to rub shoulders in service, side by side.

## SARA

At the same time this was happening in our marriage, a man in the city was uniting churches to pray for the end of abortion in Charlotte with a ministry called Love Life. He asked our church to come to the local abortion clinic in Charlotte just to pray. That's all he wanted us to do: pray.

When I was growing up, my mom was very pro-life and a lot of that rubbed off on me. In fact, some of my best friends were young mothers and I was able to encourage them through that critical time. But I'd done that in the safety of my own environment. Now we were talking about going to an abortion clinic. That felt like a whole new level of commitment.

## CORY

It was around this time that Sara and I were digging into the book of James and hearing that we needed to be doers of the word, not just hearers. So I said, "We're supposed to do this. So let's go and do it."

## SARA

As soon as we arrived, we started praying. When we rounded the corner, we saw a line of cars at the clinic. It looked to me like a line at a fast food drive-through, with women trying to get into the clinic. Car after car, all lined up, ready to take their orders.

I kept staring at that line. Car after car meant dead baby after dead baby. Murder after murder. Hurting mother after hurting mother. The reality of what was happening hit me hard.

I started sobbing. I looked over at Cory and he was crying too. I remember thinking, "I can't do nothing. I can't just sit here turning a blind eye to it and say this is not for me. This is not what I'm supposed to be doing when I know what's going on, and I know how my mother raised me."

I needed to be here helping these moms, interacting with them, talking to them about God's love. I needed to do more! Praying on the sidewalk was fine, but God wanted me to be the hands and feet, eyes and mouth of His love—and His love acts!

That's when we got involved with Cities4Life, a sidewalk counseling ministry that provides mothers-to-be with truth, assurance, and a sonogram so they can see the face of their child.

## CORY

We decided to become sidewalk counselors together. Instead of being separated (or even divorced), we were now united in purpose to connect heaven to earth for needy mothers seeking abortion. It was our destiny … together.

During that time, we met up with a 16-year-old girl named Precious. We encountered her on Mother's Day at the abortion clinic—that's right—Mother's Day.

Sara and I were standing on the corner, maybe 200 or 300 feet away from the cars, and we saw these two pro-abortion advocates marching toward us. *Uh-oh,* we thought. *Confrontation ahead.* We didn't want to fight. We wanted to love, so we moved away and found ourselves right in front of this car that stopped, and this girl named Precious stepped out.

Her mom—unfortunately, you read that correctly—her mom had driven Precious two and a half hours to get an abortion that day. As we talked with her, we could tell Precious didn't really want to do this. She kept glancing at her mom for help with the final decision to walk twenty yards to her baby's death. We kept pleading with her about the love of Jesus and this beautiful baby, and we reminded her that it was Mother's Day.

Her mom said very little, but the tears on her face said it all. We gave Precious a handbook on the development of a baby, detailing the abortion procedure, covering all the emotions that women have felt after an abortion. Yet with all that, she still responded with no emotion. It was a struggle to break through.

At just that time, 400 people from Love Life on the other side of the street filled the air with hymns and prayers while we were sharing the Gospel with Precious and her mom. The power of all those people surrounding her with love mirrored the love of God's arms around her, telling Precious she was safe. I said to her, "We have all these Christian brothers and sisters, united in Christ, ready to link arms with you through this. You are not alone in this situation."

She continued to stare blankly while her mom sobbed and sobbed.

## SARA

Then Flip Benham walked up. Flip isn't just David and Jason's dad. He's THE guy when it comes to the pro-life movement. He's counseled thousands of women and saved thousands of babies. He walked up and assessed the situation, watching how Precious kept glancing at her mom.

Flip said, "Mom, she's looking to you. She wants to know that you are there to help her. She needs your help. She needs your approval. She's looking to you, Mom." That's when they both burst out crying, sobbing loudly and just hugging each other. Flip's truthful words became a turning point where their hearts turned back toward each other to make this decision as a family. They were going to choose life for this baby.

Heaven touched earth at that moment.

We went with them so that Precious could get a free ultrasound and she was able to see her beautiful 13-week-old baby. Then we plugged them into a local pregnancy care center. Because they didn't go to church, we found a local church to help them as well.

As we finished and said our goodbyes, I said, "Happy Mother's Day, Precious." She smiled, which I hadn't seen much of that day, and said, "Thank you." As they left, mother and daughter were smiling and laughing. You could see the joy, the transformation in their hearts and minds—in this whole situation. Heaven's love invaded their lives that day.

I followed up with them afterward. In one of our texts, Precious said, "Thank you so much for stopping me from making the worst decision ever. I'm so thankful for all the encouraging words of God."

## CORY

For us, we became a bridge to be used by God the moment we agreed to make our marriage work on His principles. Satan wanted to ruin our marriage. God wanted to rebuild it for a greater good—literally bringing life instead of death to us and those around us.

As a result of that restoration, we got involved in the pro-life movement, and together, we're helping connect heaven to earth—first for Precious and her little baby and for countless mothers since then. God not only saved a marriage, but He also saved a "precious" life and many more to come.

# CHAPTER 27

# CAN I BORROW YOUR KEYS?

We used to break into houses for a living—at least, that's what we had to do in our first business. We started a real estate company that managed and sold foreclosed houses for banks. When a bank took a house back from a client in default, they'd call us to help them get it fixed up to sell. But first, we had to get inside. If no one lived there, we had to find a way to get in. So—we broke in. Well, technically it wasn't breaking in because we had permission from the bank, but it feels cool and edgy to say we broke in.

Once inside, we had to take pictures of all the rooms, as well as make a list of all the stuff left in the house. We learned quickly that walking through a dark, empty house with no electricity, full of junk was not for the faint of heart. Scenes from every scary movie we'd watched as kids came flooding back as we crept down the hallway praying nobody would jump out of the closet wearing a hockey mask.

Basements were the worst. It's sad to admit, but there were times we were so scared we refused to go down to the basement unless we were together. One of us would hold the flashlight while the other held the camera.

"We know you're in there!" we'd yell at the top of our lungs, voices shaking. "So just get out!"

Don't judge us. You would've done the same thing!

Fortunately for us, as our company grew, we hired people to do all this for us. If you remember Frankie, Tori's brother, from the previous chapter, he was one of our first agents who inspected houses for us. A pretty forgetful guy, he left his flashlight at the office one time when he had to get a full set of pictures in a windowless basement. Talk about freaky. He was forced to snap a picture and use the flash so he could see what was in front of him before walking to the next room. He tiptoed from room to room, feeling at any moment someone was going to jump out and grab him. To take the last picture, he had to open a closet door in the far corner of the room. So, he creaked the door open (not able to see anything at all) aimed his camera at the darkness and snapped a pic. The second his flash went off he saw a person standing there, staring right at him. He almost had a heart attack on the spot.

He took off running across the room, up the stairs and bolted out the front door. He jumped over the porch rail, ran through the bushes, and lunged into his car, looking behind him to see if the guy was chasing him. But no one was there. Barely able to breathe and still not feeling his legs, he took out his camera to see exactly what it was he saw. And to his surprise—it was a life-sized cardboard cut out of Captain Spock from Star Trek.

When he came back to the office that day, we heckled him pretty hard. Such were the tales of our life in the foreclosure business.

When we first started fixing up foreclosures, we decided not to hire a locksmith to handle the lock changes. We were starving boys working in an all-commission business, so we chose to handle breaking and entering ourselves to make a little extra money.

As scary as it sometimes was, it worked out great, until the day I (David) showed up to a house that appeared to be vacant. When I drilled out the knob on the front door and walked in I discovered a dude singing in the shower down the hall while the television was on in the living room. He never even heard me drill out the lock.

I had no idea what to do—I didn't want to get shot—so I slowly backed out the door, quietly closed it and left a brand-new knob set on his front porch. I can't imagine what went through his mind as he walked into his living room and saw the hole in his front door where there used to be a knob. A few weeks later, he was out of the house and I was able to change all the locks, but it was scary there at the beginning.

## KEYS

Some people we encounter are like those locked houses. They belong to God, they just don't know it yet. We're eager to help them connect with God, yet they've shut us—and all believers—out. The good news is we've already been given the keys to those hearts. We believe that's what Jesus is talking about when He says in the Gospels He's giving believers the "keys to the Kingdom" (Matthew 16:19). And although the disciples at the time thought that meant power on an earthly level—like government—it turned out he meant something more practical and deeply relational.

Our good friend and brilliant theologian, Dr. Tony Evans, describes these keys as "Biblical truths applied to a relevant life situation."[1] When God wants to bring heaven to earth in someone's life, He gives us Biblical truths to apply to the exact situation. And the only way we get the keys is to walk in love. It's the most important thing—"Most important of all, continue to show deep love for each other, for love covers a multitude of sins" (1 Peter 4:8).

Love unlocks the heart. When we walk in love, God gives us the truths we need that can open even the tightest locked heart. Of course, we know the Holy Spirit is the one who does the work and some people reject Him, but our responsibility remains the same—love people and use the keys (truths) God gives us to bring His presence into the home of their heart.

Keys represent authority, and if we refuse to operate in love, we won't have the authority to act on God's behalf. He can't give us the key to people's hearts until we see people the way He does.

---

[1]Evans, Tony. 2015. *Kingdom Man: Every Man's Destiny, Every Woman's Dream.* *Colorado Springs, CO: Focus on the Family.*

Sometimes the key to unlocking a heart may look as simple as sharing this truth: "God didn't make a mistake when He made you—He loves you and wants you to know He's right here with you." Or it may look like a small rebuke to a friend you know has stepped out of line.

Either way, when you operate out of a spirit of love for someone, God will give you the words to say and the right tone to say it. They may like it or they may not. They may break down crying or try to ram you with their grocery cart. Their response is not in your control. Your responsibility is simply to put the key in the lock and turn it.

## WHAT DOES LOVE LOOK LIKE?

Different keys go into different locks. So how are we supposed to know which key to use in which situation? Well, we've discovered the best question to ask is, "What does love look like in this situation?"

This is similar to the question Tori mentioned in earlier, "what does love require of me?" Both questions are valid to get us moving in the right direction. We like using the phrase, "what does love look like" because of the vivid pictures Christ painted for us in His own life.

Two examples from His life show us what this looks like. He was always operating out of a heart of compassion toward people. But, it didn't look the same every time. There was a time when He was preaching to a crowd of 4,000, and He recognized everyone was hungry. The Bible says, "He felt love" for them, so He performed an amazing miracle and fed them all with a few loaves of bread and fish (Matthew 15:32).

Love at that moment looked like feeding people with physical food to cure the craving in their stomachs. The people loved it.

Our wives will tell you the key to our hearts is through our stomachs as well!

Before you put a box around what Christ's love looks like and the keys He used to connect people to God, consider another occasion. This time we see Jesus talking to a rich young man who wanted to know how He could have eternal life. The Bible says, "Jesus felt love for Him" (Mark 10:21). He felt genuine compassion for the man.

What Jesus did next rocks our paradigm of what love looks like. He told the man the one thing he didn't want to hear—"sell everything and give to the poor. Then you will have treasure in heaven" (Mark 10:22).

That's a bit harsh. Why did Jesus say this? Because He knew the only thing that would unlock this man's heart was full surrender to God—this was the key. His love for things kept him disconnected from God, so Jesus pointed out that if he wanted eternal life it would require from him a willingness to forsake everything.

The saddest part of the story is that it ends with the man walking away "saddened." The love of Jesus broke this man's heart (Mark 10:22). Christ showed him exactly what he needed to do to connect with his creator, but the man wasn't willing to do it. When Jesus inserted the key of surrender into his locked heart, the man pulled it back out and walked away, disconnected from the God who could have set him free.

Love doesn't always look like what we think it should. This is why it requires both brokenness and boldness—humility and courage. These working together allows us to operate in love and possess the key to unlock the hearts of people.

## LOVE IS THE CODE

In our business, we install lockboxes on the front doors to hold the keys to the house. Without the code, you don't get the keys. And without the keys, you don't get inside. But once you have the code, you get the keys. And once you have the keys, you get inside. It's really simple.

We've seen this time and again in our lives as we seek to become a bridge connecting heaven to earth for those God brings along our path. Love is the lockbox, and truth is the key. Without love, we don't get the key, and without the key, we don't get inside.

So, it's vital to walk in love—true, biblical love for God and others—so we can have direct access into the hearts of those God places along our path.

# CHAPTER 28

# THE ULTIMATE CONNECTOR

I n 2015, we were asked to participate in the K-Love Awards in Nashville, Tennessee. We had just released our first book, *Whatever the Cost*, and it was in the running for Christian book of the year. We didn't win—some no-name lady beat us out. I think her name was Lysa Terkeurst or something (HA!).

One of the highlights of our night came at the end when we ran into Louie Giglio under the raining confetti and flashing lights. While everyone was rushing to meet all the famous musicians, we made a B-line for Louie. He's always been one of our favorite speakers. The way he explains the supernatural by looking at the natural is quite a gift.

In one of his messages, he talked about a time when a molecular biologist came to shake his hand after a sermon. In the course of the conversation, the man asked him what the topic of his next sermon series was going to be. Louie responded, "It's going to be about the glory of God and the human body."

This interested the man because he was an expert in the cellular structure of the body. So, he asked Louie, "How are you going to finish out the series? What's your left hook?"

Loui admitted he wasn't sure. The man excitedly told him about a little, unknown cell adhesion molecule in the body called *laminin*. He said, "You've got to finish with laminin—it's literally the glue that holds our bodies together!" (https://www.youtube.com/watch?v=nAbVSB7BGEg).

Now, I (Jason) will pause here for a moment and say that when I heard the sermon, I immediately went to my computer and looked it up myself. I searched "Laminin" on the Internet and studied everything I could. And the more I read, the more my heart burned with excitement.

I found out our bodies are made up of billions of cells that connect to each other to function properly and make us healthy. I think I learned this in sixth-grade science, but I had already forgotten (and you probably did too!). This need for connection is where laminin comes in. Laminin is a "cell adhesion molecule" that sits outside cells and connects them to the body tissue. It also has arms that attach with other laminin molecules as they bind cells. A bunch of laminin molecules working together connect our cells to our tissue so everything stays in place for our organs to function properly (https://answersingenesis.org/biology/microbiology/laminin-and-the-cross/).

David got lost writing this with me, but simply put, laminin is the glue that holds our bodies together. Without this vital molecule connecting things, our bodies would literally fall apart.

Louie was just as impressed with this tiny molecule as I was when he researched it for himself. But the coolest part was what he said in his sermon about why this molecular biologist was so excited about laminin. He told Louie to look up its image on the Internet. When he did his mind was blown.

So, I did the same thing and clicked "images." When I saw the shape of laminin for myself I jumped on top of my bed and did a happy dance right in front of my family. Not really, but that's what happened in my heart.

Laminin is in the shape of a—wait for it—CROSS!

Dancing now.

Go put your boogie shoes on and check it out for yourself.

This has to be the most divine mic-drop of all time. You can be whatever religion you want—Buddhist, Muslim, Hindu, Atheist, Christian, whatever—but every single one of us is held together by a cross-shaped molecule that points directly to Jesus.

Long before we had the technology to see cells and molecules in our bodies Paul wrote, "He is before all things, and in Him all things hold together" (Colossians 1:17). Without Jesus, everything falls apart. When Paul says, "all things" he means ALL THINGS!

This is life changing. As you read this book your body is being held together by a God-designed molecule so small you can't see it with your naked eye and it's in the shape of a cross—the very cross to which God's Son was nailed for you.

The chief priests who pronounced Christ's crucifixion—laminin gave them the ability to speak the words. The centurions who nailed Jesus to the cross—laminin gave them the strength to drive the nails. The leaders who put the early Christians in the arena full of hungry lions—laminin gave them the power to pass the sentence.

Christ has always been there. He is our ultimate connector, in all things. Without the cross, our body, our life, the whole world falls apart.

The next time you find yourself at odds with people because they think, behave, look, or want different things from you, consider they too desperately need Jesus. And you can either stand in the *way* or stand in the *gap*. At that moment, be mindful of laminin—the tiny molecule that reveals the Cross in every one of us. And be their connection back to God.

## HIS PART OUR PART

Jesus has already done His part as the ultimate connection between heaven and earth. His work on the cross holds us together internally—figuratively and literally. We cannot exist without Him. Each of us desperately needs what Christ did on the cross—whether we know it and openly confess it or not. Jesus willingly stretched out his hands and allowed Himself to become that which He prayed about—a bridge connecting heaven to earth.

The only appropriate response to that kind of mind-blowing love, mercy, and grace is for us to do our part and share it with others. There's a dying world in desperate need of men and women of faith who are willing to stand in the gap for them.

We don't need more bullies who stand boldly for truth but are not broken over their sin.

We don't need more bystanders who are broken over their sin but refuse to stand boldly for truth.

We need people who are bold *and* broken—those who are willing to lay it all on the line to become a bridge that connects a dying world back to the God who desperately loves them. And by their lives, they become the answer to that famous prayer—"Your Kingdom come, Your will be done, on earth as it is in Heaven."

God is still looking for people who will stand in the gap today, just as He did thousands of years ago in Ezekiel's time. The question is, will you be that person? We believe you will.

Jesus has done His part.

Now it's time to do yours.

Let's do this together—let's *Stand—In—The—Gap*!